Table of Contents:

Author Page

About the Author

Copyright Page

Copyright

Disclaimer Page

Disclaimer

Chapter 1: The Nature of Money

'Understanding Money: Its Various Functions and Different Forms'

Historical Overview: The Evolution from Barter Systems to Fiat Currency

The Rise of Bitcoin

Chapter 2: The Flaws of Fiat Currency

The Detailed Mechanics of Fiat Money

Inflation: Understanding Its Causes and Consequences

The Dangers of Overprinting

Chapter 3: Historical Evolution of Money

The Gold Standard: A Comprehensive Overview of Its History and Significance

Moving from Gold to Fiat

'The Digital Revolution: The Emergence of Bitcoin'

Chapter 4: Inflation and Purchasing Power

Understanding Inflation: What It Means for Consumers

Case Studies: Historical Examples of Hyperinflation

The Diminishing Worth of Money: The Real-World Impacts of Fiat Currency at Work

Chapter 5: Bitcoin as an Inflation Hedge

The Unique Properties of Bitcoin: Scarcity, Security, and Decentralization

'Real-World Case Studies of Bitcoin Utilization in Various Inflationary Contexts'

Comparative Performance Analysis: Bitcoin in Relation to Traditional Fiat Currencies

Chapter 6: The Role of Central Bank Policies and Their Significant Impact on the Economy

The Significance of Central Banks in Shaping Monetary Policy

Quantitative Easing and Its Impact on the Value of Fiat Currency

Bitcoin's Reaction to Actions Taken by Central Banks

Chapter 7: Comparative Analysis of Investments

Conventional Investments During Times of Inflationary Economic Conditions

Bitcoin Compared to Stocks and Bonds: An Analysis of History

Diversification Strategies in an Inflationary Era

Chapter 8: Monetary Policy and Economic Crises

'The Connection Between Monetary Policy and Economic Recessions'

Case Studies: Past Crises and Their Outcomes

The Rise of Bitcoin as a Response to Policy Failures

Chapter 9: Grassroots Movements for Bitcoin Adoption

The Importance of Community in the Expansion of Bitcoin

Case Studies of Hyperinflationary Economies

Advocacy and Education: Spreading the Message

Chapter 10: Understanding Bitcoin Technology

Blockchain Technology: The Foundation of Bitcoin

    Decentralization: Implications for Trust and Security

    The Future of Blockchain Beyond Bitcoin

Chapter 11: Psychological Effects of Fiat Dependency

    Consumer Habits and Fiat Money

    The Effect of Inflation on Consumer Spending Patterns

    Shifting Mindsets: Embracing Bitcoin

Chapter 12: Future Predictions for Bitcoin

    Bitcoin's Place in the Evolving Monetary Landscape

    Potential for Bitcoin to Replace Traditional Systems

    The Role of Regulation in Bitcoin's Future

Author Page

About the Author

J. R. Glenn writes about money the way most people wish it had been explained to them the first time: clearly, directly, and without pretending the system is working better than it is.

His work focuses on financial truth, economic freedom, and the growing divide between what people are told about money and what they actually experience in real life. In *Broken Money*, he examines the cracks in fiat currency and the case for Bitcoin as an alternative worth serious attention.

J. R. Glenn writes for readers who are tired of watching their purchasing power shrink while being told everything is normal. His mission is simple: help people see the system more clearly so they can think more independently and act more wisely.

Broken Money: The Case Against Fiat and the Rise of Bitcoin

By: J. R. Glenn

Copyright 2026

Table of Contents:

Copyright Page

Copyright

Broken Money: The Case Against Fiat and the Rise of Bitcoin

Copyright © 2026 by **J. R. Glenn**

All rights reserved.

No part of this book may be reproduced, stored in a retrieval system, or transmitted in any form or by any means, including electronic, mechanical, photocopying, recording, or otherwise, without the prior written permission of the copyright holder, except for brief quotations used in reviews, articles, or other permitted uses under copyright law.

This is a work of nonfiction. The views and opinions expressed in this book are those of the author and are provided for informational and educational purposes only.

Published independently by J. R. Glenn.

Disclaimer Page

Disclaimer

This book is intended for **educational and informational purposes only**.

Nothing in this book should be construed as financial, investment, legal, tax, or accounting advice. The author is not acting as your financial advisor, attorney, accountant, or licensed investment professional. You should consult a qualified professional before making any financial or investment decisions.

The author has made every reasonable effort to provide accurate and up-to-date information. However, financial systems, regulations, markets, technologies, and economic conditions change over time, and no guarantee is made regarding the completeness, accuracy, or current applicability of the material presented.

Any discussion of Bitcoin, fiat currency, inflation, investing, wealth preservation, or monetary policy reflects the author's opinions, analysis, and interpretation of publicly available information. Past performance does not guarantee future results. All investments involve risk, including the possible loss of principal.

The reader accepts full responsibility for any actions taken based on the information in this book.

Chapter 1: The Nature of Money

'Understanding Money: Its Various Functions and Different Forms'

Defining money requires a comprehensive understanding of its essential functions and various forms throughout the course of history. Money serves three fundamental functions: as a medium of exchange, a unit of account, and a store of value. Historically, numerous commodities such as gold and silver effectively fulfilled these roles, providing not only tangible value but also a sense of stability in economic transactions. However, as societies and economies evolved over time, governments began to introduce fiat currencies. These currencies are not backed by any physical commodities; rather, their value relies on the trust and confidence placed in the authority that issues them. This significant shift has brought about profound changes in the way individuals perceive value, engage in economic transactions, and make decisions regarding spending and investing. Consequently, this transformation has had a lasting influence on consumer behavior and investment strategies in the modern financial landscape.

The historical evolution of money intricately highlights the significant transition from tangible assets, such as precious metals, to increasingly abstract representations of value. Gold, long revered for its inherent scarcity and intrinsic value, served as the backbone of early economic systems, establishing a foundation for trade and commerce. However, the introduction of paper money marked a pivotal change, and ultimately, the advent of digital currencies further transformed the landscape of financial transactions in unprecedented ways. While fiat currency undeniably provided greater convenience and efficiency in everyday transactions, it also introduced new vulnerabilities, particularly the risk of inflation stemming from excessive printing and increases in supply. This situation has led to a growing skepticism among both investors and consumers regarding the long-term viability and stability of fiat money. As a result, this skepticism has paved the way for alternative forms of currency, such as Bitcoin, which offer unique solutions to some of the challenges posed by traditional monetary systems.

Inflation presents a considerable threat to purchasing power, effectively exposing the inherent shortcomings of fiat currency systems. As governments persist in printing excessive amounts of money to stimulate their economies, the inevitable result is often a significant devaluation of currency, thereby diminishing the overall buying power of consumers. This troubling phenomenon is particularly pronounced in hyperinflationary economies, where the costs of basic goods and services can skyrocket dramatically, leaving ordinary citizens grappling to maintain their standard of living amidst rising prices. In stark contrast, Bitcoin introduces a deflationary economic model characterized by a capped supply, which offers a compelling potential safeguard against the erosion of value that routinely afflicts traditional fiat currency systems. By limiting the total number of coins that can ever be mined, Bitcoin aims to preserve value over time, providing consumers with a more stable alternative.

Bitcoin has emerged as a compelling and increasingly relevant hedge against inflation, with numerous real-world case studies illustrating its remarkable resilience during various economic downturns. Investors have turned to Bitcoin with greater frequency during periods of monetary instability, recognizing its unique potential to effectively preserve wealth in challenging times. Comparative analyses demonstrate that Bitcoin often outperforms traditional investments during inflationary periods, which attracts a growing number of individuals who are actively seeking to protect their assets from the eroding effects of inflation. This ongoing trend underscores the growing recognition of Bitcoin not merely as a speculative asset but as a genuinely viable alternative to fiat money, especially in uncertain economic climates where traditional financial systems may falter.

The influence of central bank policies on the value of fiat currencies is significant, impacting various crucial factors such as interest rates, inflation expectations, and overall economic stability. As central banks increasingly pursue expansive monetary policies to stimulate growth, the consequences for fiat currencies become more pronounced and evident in the global marketplace. The emergence of Bitcoin, combined with grassroots efforts that actively promote its use and acceptance, indicates a notable shift in consumer attitudes and preferences towards alternative financial systems. As individuals and businesses alike seek out alternatives to the conventional monetary system, the underlying technology behind Bitcoin, particularly innovations such as blockchain and the principles of decentralization, presents a compelling and encouraging solution. This shift could potentially lead to a financial future in which Bitcoin not only coexists with but could fundamentally replace outdated fiat systems, offering a more resilient and transparent monetary framework.

Historical Overview: The Evolution from Barter Systems to Fiat Currency

The evolution of money has been a transformative journey that has profoundly shaped human civilization. It began with the barter system, where goods and services were exchanged directly without a standardized medium of exchange. This system, while functional in its simplicity, posed significant challenges, including the double coincidence of wants. This concept required both parties involved in the transaction to desire exactly what the other had to offer, making exchanges complicated and often unfeasible. As societies grew in complexity and trade expanded across regions, the inherent limitations of barter became increasingly evident. This realization led to the introduction of commodity money, including valuable items such as gold and silver, which offered a more efficient and practical means of conducting transactions. These precious metals not only held intrinsic value due to their rarity and desirability but were also widely accepted across different cultures and regions. This acceptance laid the groundwork for the broader concept of money as a reliable store of value, paving the way for the development of more sophisticated financial systems that we rely on today.

The transition from commodity money to fiat currency marked a substantial and transformative shift in the monetary landscape that has significantly influenced economic systems worldwide. Fiat money, which is issued by governments and derives its value from the trust and confidence of the public rather than any inherent intrinsic value, quickly became the dominant and preferred form of currency in many societies. This shift was facilitated by the growing need for a more flexible and responsive monetary system capable of adapting to the complexities and fluctuations of economic changes and challenges. However, as governments began to overprint and excessively issue fiat currency in response to various economic pressures, inflation emerged as a persistent and concerning issue, eroding purchasing power and diminishing the overall value of savings for individuals and businesses alike. This troubling phenomenon has raised significant alarm among investors, consumers, and economists, highlighting the inherent vulnerabilities of fiat systems and prompting a critical reevaluation of money's role and function in the broader economy.

Inflation has increasingly emerged as a central concern for consumers who rely on fiat currency, as it has a direct and significant impact on their ability to effectively purchase goods and services in daily life. Historical trends clearly illustrate how inflation can spiral out of control, particularly during times of economic distress, political instability, or mismanagement of monetary policy by governing bodies. As a result, the purchasing power of fiat currencies steadily declines over time, leading to a troubling cycle of rising prices coupled with stagnant wages. This challenging economic environment has prompted many individuals, families, and investors to actively seek out alternatives that can better preserve their value against inflation. Consequently, there has been a notable surge of interest in cryptocurrencies, particularly Bitcoin, which is specifically designed to be deflationary and inherently resistant to various inflationary pressures that plague traditional currency systems.

Bitcoin emerges as a compelling hedge against inflation, with numerous real-world case studies showcasing its effectiveness in hyperinflationary economies around the globe. Countries such as Venezuela and Zimbabwe have experienced the devastating impacts of runaway inflation on their fiat currencies, leading to severe economic challenges for their citizens. In these challenging contexts, Bitcoin has offered a viable alternative, empowering individuals to retain their value and conduct transactions outside of the traditional monetary system that has failed them. The decentralized nature of Bitcoin, combined with its capped supply and resistance to government control, positions it as a particularly robust asset amidst economic uncertainty. This unique combination has attracted significant attention not only from investors seeking new opportunities but also from grassroots movements advocating for its wider adoption as a means of financial empowerment and stability in times of crisis.

Central bank policies play a crucial role in shaping the value of fiat currency, often leading to a range of unintended consequences that can destabilize economies in various ways. As central banks implement expansive monetary policies, such as quantitative easing and low-interest rates, the risk of inflation escalates significantly, further diminishing public trust in fiat systems. This backdrop of economic turmoil and uncertainty has driven many investors to explore Bitcoin and other cryptocurrencies as viable alternative investments. A detailed comparative analysis reveals that during inflationary periods, Bitcoin has often outperformed traditional investment assets like stocks and bonds, thereby solidifying its status as a potential replacement for conventional monetary systems. As the landscape of money continues to evolve rapidly, understanding the historical context and implications of these shifts is essential for both investors and crypto enthusiasts alike, enabling them to navigate the complexities of modern financial systems effectively.

The Rise of Bitcoin

The emergence of Bitcoin can be traced back to the significant financial turmoil of the late 2000s, a period marked by rampant inflation, extensive bank bailouts, and a growing sense of distrust towards traditional financial systems. The catastrophic 2008 financial crisis served as a powerful catalyst for a new form of money that promised to effectively circumvent the numerous pitfalls associated with fiat currency. Satoshi Nakamoto, the mysterious and pseudonymous creator of Bitcoin, introduced a revolutionary decentralized digital currency that operates on a robust peer-to-peer network, allowing users to engage in transactions directly without needing intermediaries or third parties. This groundbreaking innovation was not merely a technological breakthrough; it represented a profound and fundamental shift in how individuals could perceive, utilize, and interact with money in an increasingly unstable and unpredictable economic environment.

Bitcoin's design fundamentally contrasts with that of fiat money, which is often subject to inflation due to excessive printing and manipulation by governments. While fiat currencies rely heavily on the confidence instilled by governmental institutions, Bitcoin stands out by offering a fixed supply that is capped at 21 million coins. This unique characteristic provides a significant hedge against inflationary pressures that can erode purchasing power over time. The property of scarcity inherent in Bitcoin is reminiscent of historical forms of money, such as gold, which has been widely regarded as a reliable store of value throughout history. As more investors and crypto enthusiasts began to understand the implications of Bitcoin's supply dynamics, it became increasingly clear that this digital asset could serve as a more dependable alternative to traditional fiat currencies, which continually struggle with the risk of losing purchasing power in the face of economic challenges.

Central banks have played a crucial and influential role in shaping the value of fiat currencies through their various monetary policies. The growing tendency to resort to quantitative easing and other expansionary measures has resulted in significant debasement of currencies across the globe. The consequences of these policies are becoming increasingly visible in everyday life, as consumers find their money losing value at an alarming and distressing rate. Bitcoin, on the other hand, operates independently of the influence exerted by central banks, allowing its holders to effectively preserve their wealth in the face of systemic failures and economic instability. Real-world case studies from countries grappling with hyperinflation, such as Venezuela and Zimbabwe, powerfully highlight how grassroots movements have turned to Bitcoin as a vital lifeline, empowering individuals to take action and protect their financial futures against the devastating effects of their governments' monetary mismanagement and irresponsible fiscal policies.

Comparative analysis of Bitcoin and traditional investments during inflationary periods reveals Bitcoin's remarkable resilience and significant potential for growth. Unlike stocks and bonds, which can be adversely affected by rising interest rates and broader economic instability, Bitcoin has often demonstrated a tendency to appreciate in value when fiat currencies face considerable devaluation. This distinctive performance has attracted a diverse range of investors, all seeking to diversify their portfolios and effectively hedge against inflationary pressures. As an increasing number of individuals recognize the numerous advantages that Bitcoin offers, its widespread adoption continues to gain momentum, indicating a broader and more pronounced shift in investment strategies that prioritize long-term stability and security over short-term gains and speculative interests.

Understanding the technology behind Bitcoin, particularly the concepts of blockchain and decentralization, is absolutely crucial for fully appreciating its profound significance in the modern financial landscape. The blockchain functions as a transparent and immutable ledger, ensuring that all transactions are recorded and verified without the need for any central authority. This decentralization not only enhances security but also fosters a strong sense of trust among users, ultimately creating a system that is resistant to manipulation and fraud. As consumers become increasingly aware of the psychological effects associated with their dependence on fiat currency, the appeal of Bitcoin as a sustainable alternative to traditional forms of money grows stronger and more compelling. Future predictions suggest that Bitcoin's potential to replace traditional monetary systems is not merely a speculative notion but rather a tangible evolution in how society perceives and interacts with money in both everyday transactions and larger economic frameworks.

Chapter 2: The Flaws of Fiat Currency

The Detailed Mechanics of Fiat Money

Fiat money operates on a fundamental principle: it derives its value from government decree rather than any intrinsic value, such as that found in precious metals like gold or silver. This system emerged and evolved as societies gradually moved away from traditional commodity-based currencies, relying increasingly on trust in the authority that issues the currency. Central banks, which are empowered and regulated by governments, play a crucial role in controlling the overall supply of fiat money in circulation. This control can lead to inflationary pressures when excessive amounts of currency are printed without a corresponding increase in economic growth. Such a dynamic becomes problematic, as it can significantly erode purchasing power over time. This erosion leaves consumers and investors exposed and vulnerable to rising prices and economic instability, potentially undermining the overall health of the economy. The ramifications of these inflationary pressures can be profound, affecting various aspects of daily life and economic activity.

The historical evolution of money provides a fascinating illustration of the transition from tangible assets, such as gold, to more abstract forms like fiat currency. Gold was highly valued for its scarcity and inherent qualities, which made it a reliable medium of exchange for centuries. However, as economies expanded and became increasingly complex, the need for more flexible and efficient monetary systems became increasingly apparent. In response to this need, fiat money was introduced as a more manageable alternative, allowing for easier transactions and facilitating trade across broader and more diverse markets. Despite its advantages, the reliance on centralized authorities to manage this system has led to numerous financial crises. These crises have been particularly pronounced during periods of economic downturn, where excessive printing of money has resulted in hyperinflation, eroding the purchasing power of citizens and diminishing trust in the currency itself.

Inflation has become a significant and pressing concern for consumers everywhere, as it directly affects their purchasing power in fundamental ways. The gradual and often persistent increase in prices means that a fixed amount of fiat currency buys less and less over time, effectively punishing diligent savers while rewarding those who hold debts. This steady decline in value is frequently exacerbated by central bank policies that tend to prioritize short-term economic stimulus measures over the more crucial need for long-term financial stability. As inflation continues to erode the real value of fiat money, many individuals are increasingly turning to alternative assets for protection, with Bitcoin emerging as a prominent option. Bitcoin is often viewed as a safeguard against the devaluation of currency and a hedge against inflation, attracting those who seek to preserve their wealth in uncertain economic times.

Bitcoin presents a compelling case as a hedge against inflation, particularly in environments where fiat currencies are failing or losing their value rapidly. Real-world case studies from countries grappling with hyperinflation, such as Venezuela and Zimbabwe, powerfully illustrate how increased Bitcoin adoption can provide a crucial lifeline for citizens striving to protect and preserve their wealth amid economic turmoil. These grassroots movements not only highlight a growing awareness but also reflect a strong desire for viable alternatives to unstable fiat systems. Bitcoin's limited supply and decentralized nature offer a stark contrast to the unpredictable inflationary consequences associated with traditional fiat money, thereby reinforcing its appeal as a solution for those affected by economic instability.

Central banks play a crucial role in the value of fiat currencies through their monetary policies, which can have profound effects on economic stability. During inflationary periods, traditional investments often struggle to maintain value, while Bitcoin has shown resilience and even appreciation in the face of economic uncertainty. The technological foundation of Bitcoin, rooted in blockchain and decentralization, empowers individuals by providing an alternative to the traditional banking system. As we look to the future, the potential for Bitcoin to replace conventional monetary systems becomes increasingly plausible, driven by a collective recognition of the flaws inherent in fiat currencies and the growing demand for a more stable and trustworthy financial alternative.

Inflation: Understanding Its Causes and Consequences

Inflation is a persistent and often troubling increase in the prices of goods and services, which erodes purchasing power and undermines the overall stability of fiat currencies. The primary causes of inflation can typically be traced back to an excessive money supply, which is often the result of central banks engaging in quantitative easing or adopting other types of expansionary monetary policies. When governments decide to print more money in an effort to stimulate the economy, they inadvertently dilute the value of the existing currency in circulation. This phenomenon has been evident in various historical contexts, ranging from the hyperinflation that plagued Weimar Germany in the early 20th century to more recent episodes in countries like Venezuela and Zimbabwe, where irresponsible overprinting of money led to catastrophic economic consequences and social unrest. Such instances serve as stark reminders of the dangers associated with mismanaged monetary policies and their long-lasting effects on national economies.

The consequences of inflation are extremely profound and far-reaching, particularly for consumers who heavily rely on fiat currency for their daily financial transactions and purchases. As prices continue to rise steadily, individuals soon discover that their savings buy significantly less than they used to, leading to a notable decrease in their overall purchasing power. This challenging situation often compels households to carefully adjust their spending habits, placing a higher priority on essential goods and services while simultaneously cutting back on discretionary expenses that are not immediately necessary. Furthermore, inflation can create a pervasive sense of uncertainty in financial markets, making it increasingly challenging for investors to accurately predict future returns on traditional assets. This unpredictability and instability drive some individuals toward exploring alternative forms of money, such as Bitcoin, which is often perceived as a potential safe haven that promises a more stable store of value in turbulent economic times.

Bitcoin's emergence as a potential hedge against inflation has garnered substantial attention, particularly in economic environments where fiat currencies are experiencing rapid devaluation. Real-world case studies provide compelling evidence of Bitcoin's resilience in various hyperinflationary scenarios, where individuals have increasingly turned to digital currencies as a means to preserve their wealth and financial stability. For instance, in countries like Argentina, citizens have progressively adopted Bitcoin as a safeguard against the significant depreciation of their national currency, seeking alternatives to protect their savings. The decentralized nature of Bitcoin empowers individuals to bypass traditional banking systems entirely, offering a viable and innovative alternative for those who are actively seeking to shield their assets from the adverse effects of inflationary pressures.

Central bank policies play a crucial role in shaping the value of fiat currencies, as the actions undertaken by these institutions have a significant and direct impact on the money supply and prevailing interest rates. When central banks decide to implement loose monetary policies, they may inadvertently contribute to inflationary pressures, which can erode consumer confidence and trust in their national currency. This diminished trust can lead consumers and investors alike to seek alternatives, such as cryptocurrencies like Bitcoin, which are not subject to the same influences as traditional centralized financial systems. A detailed comparison of Bitcoin's performance against traditional investments during periods of inflation reveals that Bitcoin often outperforms conventional assets, highlighting its potential as a resilient and attractive investment option in times of economic uncertainty and instability.

The rise of Bitcoin has significantly catalyzed grassroots movements that advocate for its widespread adoption, particularly in hyperinflationary economies where traditional financial systems have faltered. These movements strongly emphasize the crucial need for financial independence and highlight the empowering potential of Bitcoin for individuals living in regions where fiat currencies have failed to maintain their value. A deeper understanding of the underlying technology of Bitcoin, especially the principles of blockchain and decentralization, further illustrates its numerous advantages over conventional monetary systems. As global awareness continues to grow regarding the psychological effects of dependency on fiat currencies, an increasing number of consumers are likely to embrace Bitcoin as a legitimate and viable alternative to the traditional financial framework. Future predictions indicate that Bitcoin could play an instrumental role in transforming existing monetary systems, ultimately offering a stable and inflation-resistant option for both investors and consumers, thereby reshaping the landscape of finance in the years to come.

The Dangers of Overprinting

The dangers of overprinting currency are vividly illustrated in the context of fiat money, where central banks frequently resort to the practice of printing more money to address various economic challenges. This approach, while intended to stimulate economic growth and alleviate financial pressures, invariably leads to inflation and a significant devaluation of purchasing power. When governments engage in printing money without corresponding economic growth or productivity increases, they effectively dilute the value of the existing currency. This creates a troubling scenario where consumers find their savings eroded and prices continuously rising, making it increasingly difficult for them to maintain their standard of living. Furthermore, investors and crypto enthusiasts must recognize that overprinting is not merely a financial issue but rather a fundamental systemic flaw inherent in fiat currency systems. This is one of the key issues that Bitcoin seeks to address through its fixed supply and decentralized nature, aiming to provide a more stable alternative.

Historically, money has undergone a significant evolution, transitioning from tangible assets like gold to the more intangible and often mismanaged fiat currencies that dominate our modern financial landscape today. Gold, recognized for its inherent scarcity and enduring value, provided a stable and reliable foundation for monetary systems throughout history. In stark contrast, fiat currency relies heavily on trust in government institutions, a trust that can be easily compromised by irresponsible and reckless monetary policies. Over the last century, numerous historical instances have vividly illustrated how excessive money printing can lead to devastating hyperinflation and ultimately, economic collapse. As central banks increasingly adopt these unsustainable practices, the pressing question arises: can Bitcoin, with its fixed supply, decentralized nature, and innovative technology, serve as a viable and sustainable alternative to this flawed and precarious financial system that we currently face?

Inflation, primarily driven by the excessive overprinting of money, has a direct and profound impact on consumer behavior and overall purchasing power. As the prices of goods and services continue to rise, consumers find themselves compelled to allocate a larger portion of their income towards essential items, which consequently leaves them with significantly less available for savings or investment opportunities. This erosion of purchasing power is particularly detrimental to individuals who are on fixed incomes or possess limited financial literacy, as they are frequently the most vulnerable segments of society during economic fluctuations. In this context, Bitcoin emerges as a compelling hedge against such rampant inflation, providing a store of value that remains largely insulated from the same inflationary pressures that afflict fiat currencies. Real-world case studies from various countries grappling with hyperinflation vividly illustrate how the adoption of Bitcoin can serve as a critical lifeline for those individuals striving to preserve their wealth and financial stability in the face of economic turmoil.

Central bank policies play a crucial role in shaping the value of fiat currencies, and the practice of overprinting often leads to a significant decline in public trust. As central banks inject increasing amounts of money into the economy, they run the risk of creating a troubling cycle of dependency on monetary stimulus, which can further destabilize financial markets and lead to unpredictable economic outcomes. In stark contrast, Bitcoin's underlying protocol is meticulously designed to resist manipulation, with its total supply strictly capped at 21 million coins. This built-in scarcity serves as a sharp contrast to the inflationary tendencies that characterize fiat currencies, making Bitcoin an increasingly appealing asset for investors who seek to protect their wealth during times of economic uncertainty and market volatility.

Grassroots movements advocating for Bitcoin adoption in hyperinflationary economies significantly underscore the growing recognition of Bitcoin as a viable solution to the pressing issues posed by rampant currency overprinting. In countries such as Venezuela and Zimbabwe, citizens have turned to Bitcoin not just as a means of transaction, but also as a crucial safeguard against the financial chaos and instability stemming from their governments' erratic monetary policies. It is imperative for investors and crypto enthusiasts to understand the technology behind Bitcoin, including its blockchain and decentralized structure, as this knowledge is essential for successfully navigating the ever-evolving landscape of cryptocurrency. As fiat currencies increasingly face scrutiny and exhibit heightened volatility, the future predictions regarding Bitcoin's potential to replace traditional monetary systems become even more compelling. This positions Bitcoin not merely as a digital asset but as a beacon of hope for a more stable and secure financial future, offering an alternative for those seeking economic resilience in uncertain times.

Chapter 3: Historical Evolution of Money

The Gold Standard: A Comprehensive Overview of Its History and Significance

The gold standard represents a pivotal moment in the extensive history of money, establishing a system in which the value of currency was directly linked to specific gold reserves. Under this significant standard, nations would issue paper money that was fully redeemable for a designated amount of gold, thereby creating a stable and predictable monetary environment that fostered trust among users. This framework effectively curtailed the arbitrary expansion of the money supply, as governments were strictly limited by their available gold holdings. Investors, economists, and crypto enthusiasts often look back at this influential era to better understand the enduring principles of sound money and to analyze the adverse effects and challenges posed by fiat currencies that have emerged since the widespread abandonment of the gold standard.

Historically, the transition from the gold standard to fiat currency marked a significant and transformative shift in monetary policy that reshaped economic landscapes. As countries gradually moved away from gold backing, they began to fully embrace the newfound flexibility of printing unlimited amounts of money without the constraints of physical reserves. This monumental change catalyzed the rise of inflation, which in turn eroded purchasing power and led to the financial instability that many economies continue to face today. The historical evolution of money serves as a compelling illustration of how the removal of tangible value from currency has resulted in recurrent cycles of boom and bust, leaving consumers increasingly vulnerable to the unpredictable whims of central banks and fluctuating government policies. This progression underscores the profound impact that monetary decisions can have on everyday lives and the overall economic environment.

Inflation has emerged as a critical and pressing concern within the fiat monetary system, directly affecting and diminishing the purchasing power of consumers across the board. Unlike the strict constraints and limitations imposed by the gold standard, fiat money can be printed without any limit or restraint, leading to a significant devaluation of currency over time. As a result, investors frequently find themselves grappling with rising costs and a decreased value of their savings, as central banks often prioritize short-term economic stimulus measures over long-term financial stability and health. This ongoing reality highlights and underscores the argument that fiat currencies are inherently flawed and problematic, making a compelling case for exploring and considering alternatives like Bitcoin, which offers a decentralized and deflationary monetary model that stands in stark contrast to traditional fiat systems.

Bitcoin has gained considerable prominence as a hedge against inflation, with numerous real-world case studies emphasizing its remarkable resilience during various economic downturns. Countries grappling with severe hyperinflation, such as Venezuela and Zimbabwe, have witnessed their populations increasingly turning to Bitcoin as a means of preserving wealth and facilitating everyday transactions. These grassroots movements illustrate the potential of Bitcoin, not only as a lucrative investment but also as a vital lifeline in extremely challenging economic circumstances. The widespread adoption of Bitcoin in these difficult environments highlights its exceptional ability to maintain value when traditional currencies fail, thereby underscoring its position as a highly viable alternative to conventional fiat currencies in the global financial landscape.

The role of central bank policies in shaping the value of fiat currency cannot be overstated, as their influence extends to various aspects of the economy. As monetary policy becomes increasingly expansive, the consequences for consumers and businesses are dire, leading to diminished trust in traditional financial systems and institutions. In contrast, Bitcoin operates independently of central banks and government regulations, utilizing blockchain technology to ensure transparency, security, and decentralization. As investors and crypto enthusiasts navigate the complexities and uncertainties of inflationary periods, a comparative analysis of Bitcoin and traditional investments reveals a growing preference for digital assets among a diverse range of investors. The future predictions regarding Bitcoin's potential to replace or supplement traditional monetary systems suggest a transformative shift in how value is stored, exchanged, and perceived, challenging the very foundations of fiat currencies while offering hope for a more stable, resilient, and equitable economic landscape for future generations.

Moving from Gold to Fiat

Transitioning from gold to fiat marked an exceptionally significant shift in the complex evolution of money, fundamentally altering both economic landscapes and consumer behavior in profound ways. Gold, long revered for its intrinsic value and scarcity, served as a reliable store of wealth for centuries, providing a sense of stability and trust. However, as economies expanded significantly and global trade intensified, the inherent limitations of physical gold became increasingly apparent. Fiat currency emerged as a practical solution to these challenges, enabling governments to issue money without the constraints imposed by physical backing. This transition was initially seen as a modernizing move, ushering in new possibilities for economic growth and flexibility. Yet, as history unfolded, the inherent flaws of fiat systems began to surface, exposing vulnerabilities and instabilities that continue to plague economies around the world today, raising questions about the long-term sustainability of such systems.

The problem with fiat currency lies in its inherent susceptibility to inflation, which is often a direct consequence of excessive printing and an unchecked increase in supply. Central banks frequently resort to measures such as quantitative easing and other monetary policies in a bid to stimulate economic growth. However, these strategies often lead to a significant devaluation of currency, eroding purchasing power and negatively impacting consumers. Historical examples are plentiful, ranging from the devastating hyperinflation in Weimar Germany to the more recent economic crises experienced in Venezuela and Zimbabwe. These situations illustrate how fiat currencies can fail spectacularly when mismanaged or poorly regulated. Such instances serve as cautionary tales, highlighting the urgent need for a more stable and reliable monetary alternative that can safeguard economic stability and protect consumers.

Bitcoin has emerged as a compelling and increasingly recognized hedge against inflation, capturing the attention of both investors and crypto enthusiasts alike. Unlike traditional fiat currencies, Bitcoin operates under a capped supply, which effectively safeguards its value against the inflationary tendencies that often plague conventional currencies. Real-world case studies, particularly in hyperinflationary economies, vividly demonstrate Bitcoin's remarkable resilience as a store of value over time. For instance, during Venezuela's severe economic collapse, countless citizens turned to Bitcoin and various cryptocurrencies as vital lifelines, successfully preserving their wealth when the local currency became virtually worthless and entirely unreliable. These compelling examples highlight Bitcoin's potential not only as a valuable investment opportunity but also as an essential means of financial survival during turbulent and uncertain times.

The impact of central bank policies on the value of fiat currency cannot be overstated. Central banks, which are responsible for regulating the monetary supply, often grapple with conflicting objectives, such as the need to stimulate economic growth while simultaneously controlling inflation. Their decisions can lead to unpredictable market reactions that further destabilize consumer confidence and create uncertainty in the financial landscape. In contrast, Bitcoin operates independently of any central bank interventions, providing a decentralized alternative that appeals to individuals who are increasingly disillusioned with traditional monetary systems and the limitations they impose. As central banks continue to navigate complex economic crises and uncertainties, the contrast between fiat currencies and Bitcoin becomes increasingly pronounced. Many investors are beginning to view Bitcoin as a reliable safe haven, particularly during times of economic instability and market volatility, further underscoring its appeal as a digital asset in a rapidly changing financial world.

The grassroots movements advocating for Bitcoin adoption in hyperinflationary economies underscore a growing and significant recognition of cryptocurrency's essential role in the modern financial landscape. With a deeper and more comprehensive understanding of blockchain technology and its inherently decentralized nature, consumers are increasingly beginning to challenge the long-standing psychological dependence on fiat currencies. As they take the time to explore the numerous benefits of Bitcoin, these movements are empowering individuals to reclaim and take control over their financial futures. Looking ahead, the potential for Bitcoin to not only replace traditional monetary systems is not just a mere possibility; it reflects a much broader shift towards alternative forms of value that prioritize stability, security, and resilience in an ever-changing and unpredictable economic environment.

'The Digital Revolution: The Emergence of Bitcoin'

The birth of Bitcoin in 2009 marked a pivotal moment in the ongoing evolution of money, presenting a significant challenge to the existing fiat currency systems that have dominated the financial landscape for decades without interruption. Bitcoin emerged from the complex backdrop of the 2008 financial crisis, a period characterized by rampant inflation, an economic downturn, and a profound loss of faith in traditional banking systems. Its inception was driven by a strong desire for a decentralized currency that could operate independently of government control and manipulation, effectively addressing the inherent weaknesses and vulnerabilities of fiat money, which has long been plagued by overprinting and diminishing purchasing power. This innovative digital currency sought to provide a viable alternative, fostering a new era in financial transactions and personal sovereignty.

Historically, money has undergone a significant evolution, transitioning from tangible assets such as gold to more abstract representations of value, including paper currency. Gold has been long revered for its scarcity, durability, and intrinsic value; however, as societies progressed and economies expanded, the need for more efficient and practical transactional mediums became apparent. This led to the widespread adoption of fiat currency, which is backed by government decree rather than by physical commodities or precious metals. While this shift facilitated easier trade and commerce, it has also introduced systemic vulnerabilities, especially during periods of excessive growth in the money supply. Such inflationary periods can erode consumer purchasing power, diminishing the value of money held by individuals. In response to these concerns, Bitcoin emerged, with its capped supply of 21 million coins. It was specifically designed to counteract these inflationary pressures, offering a deflationary alternative to the ever-increasing supplies of fiat currency, and aiming to provide a more stable store of value in a rapidly changing economic landscape.

The failures of fiat currencies are starkly illustrated by their performance during inflationary periods, where their weaknesses become painfully evident. As governments resort to quantitative easing and various other monetary policy tools in an effort to stimulate the economy, they inadvertently dilute the value of their currencies, leading to significant devaluation. This creates a challenging scenario in which consumers find it increasingly difficult to maintain their purchasing power, ultimately resulting in heightened financial insecurity for many. In this context, Bitcoin's value proposition becomes particularly compelling, as it has the potential to serve as an effective hedge against the detrimental effects of such inflationary trends. Real-world case studies from countries grappling with hyperinflation, such as Venezuela and Zimbabwe, powerfully demonstrate how Bitcoin adoption can provide individuals with a viable means to preserve their wealth, even in the face of collapsing fiat currencies and severe economic instability.

Central bank policies play an incredibly crucial and significant role in shaping and determining the value of fiat currencies in today's economy. Actions such as interest rate adjustments, quantitative easing, and bond purchasing directly and profoundly influence inflation rates, consumer confidence, and overall economic stability. During times of economic crises and downturns, these policies often fall short of their intended goals, leading to further depreciation and erosion of fiat currencies. In stark contrast, Bitcoin's decentralized nature provides a strong buffer against the unpredictability and volatility of central bank interventions and decisions. This unique aspect has led to a detailed comparative analysis of Bitcoin versus traditional investments, particularly during inflationary periods. Such analyses reveal that while traditional assets like stocks and bonds may falter and struggle, Bitcoin has frequently outperformed as an asset class that retains its value, demonstrating resilience even in challenging economic environments.

Grassroots movements advocating for Bitcoin adoption in hyperinflationary economies underscore the currency's significant potential to disrupt established monetary systems. As individuals increasingly seek alternatives to fiat currencies that are rapidly losing value, Bitcoin's decentralized technology and robust blockchain infrastructure provide a transparent, secure, and innovative method for conducting transactions and storing wealth. A deeper understanding of the psychological effects stemming from dependence on fiat currency reveals how consumer behavior is intricately influenced by their trust in financial institutions. As faith in traditional monetary systems continues to erode, the prospects for Bitcoin as a viable and effective replacement for fiat currency become increasingly plausible, indicating a transformative shift in the future landscape of money and financial interactions. This evolution could redefine how value is perceived and exchanged, further solidifying Bitcoin's role in the global economy.

Chapter 4: Inflation and Purchasing Power

Understanding Inflation: What It Means for Consumers

Inflation is a critical economic phenomenon that directly affects consumers' purchasing power and overall financial well-being in profound ways. For investors and crypto enthusiasts, understanding inflation is not just beneficial; it is essential, especially when considering the inherent flaws of fiat currency. When central banks engage in the excessive printing of money, the value of that currency diminishes significantly, leading to a persistent rise in the prices of goods and services. This erosion of purchasing power is not merely an economic statistic; it translates into tangible consequences in everyday life, as consumers find themselves increasingly able to buy less with the same amount of money they once had. As inflation continues to rise globally, the implications for individuals and businesses become increasingly severe and far-reaching, prompting many to actively seek alternatives to traditional fiat systems in an effort to protect their financial future and maintain their standard of living.

Historically, the concept of money has undergone a remarkable evolution, transitioning from tangible assets such as gold and silver to increasingly abstract forms, including fiat currencies that are based solely on government decree and trust. This significant shift has often led to economic instability, particularly as governments have turned to extensive money printing during times of crisis and uncertainty. The reliance on fiat currencies has revealed substantial vulnerabilities, as evidenced by various economies that have suffered from hyperinflation and severe devaluation. For consumers, this troubling reality means that their hard-earned savings can swiftly lose value, eroding their purchasing power and compromising their ability to plan for the future effectively. Understanding the historical context of money is crucial, as it underscores the pressing necessity for a more stable and reliable alternative, a role that Bitcoin aspires to fulfill in the modern financial landscape.

The failure of fiat currency to maintain its purchasing power becomes increasingly evident when one closely examines inflation rates across various economies. Consumer prices have surged dramatically in numerous countries, significantly diminishing the real value of both income and savings for individuals. As the cost of living consistently rises, the purchasing power of consumers is severely undermined, necessitating higher wages that often struggle to keep pace with the relentless tide of inflation. This ongoing cycle perpetuates a sense of economic uncertainty, making it increasingly challenging for consumers to budget effectively or save for their long-term financial goals. Consequently, many individuals are beginning to recognize that traditional fiat currency systems are not adequately equipped to safeguard their financial futures. This realization is leading to a growing interest in alternative assets such as Bitcoin, which are perceived as more reliable options for preserving wealth in an unstable economic environment.

Bitcoin presents a compelling and robust case as a hedge against inflation, offering a decentralized alternative that is inherently resistant to the inflationary pressures that frequently plague fiat currencies. Numerous real-world case studies illustrate how Bitcoin has consistently maintained its value even in hyperinflationary environments, thereby empowering individuals to effectively preserve their wealth during tumultuous economic times. In countries where traditional currencies have dramatically collapsed, the adoption of Bitcoin has surged as people increasingly seek stability and security in their financial transactions. This grassroots movement not only highlights the resilience of Bitcoin but also showcases its potential not just as a speculative investment, but as a genuinely viable solution for consumers grappling with the severe consequences of fiat currency depreciation and instability.

The dynamics of central bank policies significantly exacerbate the multifaceted challenges faced by consumers in an increasingly inflationary environment. Decisions made by central banks, which are often aimed at stimulating economic growth and activity, can inadvertently lead to a series of unintended consequences that inflate the money supply and dilute the value of currency over time. As investors, analysts, and crypto enthusiasts closely analyze these complex trends, they increasingly recognize that Bitcoin's fixed supply represents a stark contrast to the inflationary mechanisms inherent in fiat money systems. The potential for Bitcoin to effectively replace traditional monetary systems is becoming more widely viewed as a viable future outcome, driven not only by pressing economic necessity but also by a growing awareness of the innovative technology that underpins this revolutionary digital asset. Understanding these crucial elements is essential for successfully navigating the intricate and evolving landscape of modern finance, enabling individuals to make informed and strategic investment decisions in this rapidly changing environment.

Case Studies: Historical Examples of Hyperinflation

Hyperinflation has consistently emerged as a significant theme in the economic histories of various nations, vividly illustrating the destructive power that an uncontrolled money supply can wield and the inherent failures of fiat currencies. One of the most striking and notable examples of this phenomenon is the hyperinflation that tragically afflicted the Weimar Republic in Germany during the tumultuous early 1920s. In the aftermath of World War I, Germany found itself burdened with enormous reparations payments, leading the government to respond by printing vast and unprecedented amounts of money in an attempt to stabilize its economy. This reckless monetary policy resulted in a staggering and unprecedented increase in prices, with the cost of a simple loaf of bread soaring dramatically from an already alarming 250 marks in early 1923 to an astonishing over 200 billion marks by November of the same year. The catastrophic collapse of the currency not only obliterated personal savings but also incited widespread social unrest and turmoil, effectively demonstrating how fiat systems can falter and collapse under the overwhelming weight of excessive and irresponsible monetary policy.

Another significant case is Zimbabwe, which experienced extreme hyperinflation during the late 2000s. The Zimbabwean government, grappling with severe economic challenges and a rapidly declining agricultural sector, resorted to printing money indiscriminately and in massive quantities. By November 2008, inflation reached an astronomical rate of 89.7 sextillion percent per month, a staggering figure that reflects the depths of the crisis. Basic commodities like food and fuel became completely unaffordable for the average citizen, and the local currency lost its value almost overnight, rendering it nearly worthless. This devastating crisis forced countless Zimbabweans to turn to foreign currencies, including the US dollar and the South African rand, for daily transactions. This shift highlights the inadequacies of fiat currency in preserving value during periods of severe economic distress and showcases the lengths to which people will go to protect their purchasing power in the face of systemic financial collapse.

In Venezuela, hyperinflation has escalated to devastating levels in recent years, driven by a toxic combination of poor governance, rampant corruption, and an excessive reliance on oil revenues. The value of the Venezuelan bolívar has plummeted dramatically, with inflation rates surpassing an astonishing 1 million percent in 2018 alone. As a direct consequence, citizens have faced immense difficulties affording even the most essential items, such as food and medicine, which has led to a drastic increase in poverty levels and a significant emigration crisis. This alarming and dire situation has sparked numerous grassroots movements advocating for the adoption of Bitcoin, as more individuals seek alternative methods to escape the failures inherent in the traditional fiat currency system. The decentralized nature of Bitcoin provides a potential lifeline from the chaos of hyperinflation, presenting hope and a viable route to financial independence for countless Venezuelans grappling with this overwhelming economic disaster. Through these movements, many are exploring innovative solutions to reclaim their financial futures amidst ongoing turmoil.

The case of Yugoslavia in the early 1990s serves as a striking example of the catastrophic effects that hyperinflation can unleash on a nation. In the wake of the country's breakup, the National Bank of Yugoslavia resorted to printing vast amounts of money to cover its burgeoning budget deficit and fund military operations. This reckless monetary policy ultimately led to hyperinflation that reached its peak in January 1994, a staggering situation where prices doubled every 34 hours. As the dinar collapsed in value, citizens were left with no choice but to turn to barter and other alternative forms of exchange, as the national currency became utterly unreliable and nearly worthless. This historical example powerfully illustrates the inherent vulnerability of fiat currencies in the face of political and economic instability, reinforcing the argument for exploring and adopting alternative monetary systems such as Bitcoin, which may offer more stability and security in uncertain times.

These case studies serve as a significant cautionary tale for investors and crypto enthusiasts alike, emphasizing the inherent risks associated with fiat currencies and highlighting the profound impact that central bank policies can have on their overall value. As global economic conditions continue to fluctuate and evolve, and in light of the valuable lessons learned from historical hyperinflation events, Bitcoin emerges as a particularly compelling hedge against inflationary pressures. By thoroughly understanding the failures and shortcomings of past monetary systems, investors can better appreciate the unique potential of Bitcoin to provide essential stability and security in an increasingly uncertain financial landscape characterized by volatility and unpredictability.

The Diminishing Worth of Money: The Real-World Impacts of Fiat Currency at Work

The erosion of value in fiat currencies is an increasingly pressing and concerning issue for both investors and crypto enthusiasts alike. Fiat currency, which is defined as government-issued money that is not backed by any physical commodity, has come under significant scrutiny due to rampant inflation that often results from excessive printing and an overabundance of supply. Historically, the transition from gold-backed currencies to fiat systems marked a pivotal shift in the structure of monetary systems across the globe. While gold's finite nature provided a relatively stable store of value, the introduction of fiat currencies has allowed governments much greater leeway in formulating monetary policy, which often leads to irresponsible fiscal practices and decisions. Consequently, many currencies around the world have experienced dramatic devaluation over time, raising significant questions about the long-term sustainability of fiat as a reliable medium of exchange in the financial landscape.

Inflation is a critical issue that significantly impacts purchasing power, illustrating the ways in which fiat currency can ultimately fail consumers. The continuous and often unchecked increase in the money supply, typically justified by central banks as a necessary measure for stimulating economic growth, ultimately results in the devaluation of existing currency. For instance, the hyperinflation experienced in Zimbabwe and Venezuela serves as stark and alarming reminders of how fiat currency can collapse under conditions of mismanagement and excessive issuance. In these distressing scenarios, consumers find their hard-earned savings eroded, leading to a profound loss of trust in the currency itself. As inflation rates skyrocket, everyday goods become increasingly unaffordable, forcing individuals to seek alternative stores of value, such as commodities or even cryptocurrencies, thereby highlighting the inherent vulnerabilities and weaknesses of fiat systems in a rapidly changing economic landscape.

Bitcoin has emerged as a strong potential hedge against inflation, supported by numerous real-world examples that demonstrate its impressive resilience and utility. In countries facing hyperinflation, there has been a notable increase in Bitcoin adoption as individuals turn to this decentralized digital asset to protect their wealth and maintain financial stability. For example, in Argentina, where inflation rates have surged to alarming levels, Bitcoin has become an essential tool for people looking to shield their savings from severe devaluation and economic turmoil. This trend highlights Bitcoin's growing appeal as a viable alternative to traditional fiat currencies, particularly due to its limited supply of 21 million coins. This contrasts sharply with the unlimited and often inflationary nature of fiat currencies, which governments can produce at will. As investors seek stability amid ongoing economic challenges, Bitcoin's fixed supply makes it an attractive option for those concerned about the risks associated with fiat money and its impact on their financial security.

Central bank policies have a profound and significant impact on the overall value of fiat currencies, often exacerbating inflationary pressures through various mechanisms such as interest rate adjustments and quantitative easing measures. These monetary policies can create a vicious cycle, where attempts to stimulate economic growth inadvertently lead to higher inflation rates and a corresponding decline in consumer confidence. The psychological effects stemming from this reliance on fiat currencies can result in unpredictable and erratic consumer behavior, which further destabilizes the broader economy. In stark contrast, Bitcoin's inherently decentralized nature and its reliance on transparent blockchain technology offer a compelling alternative. This structure effectively removes the need for centralized control, thereby empowering individuals to take charge of their own financial futures and make informed decisions without the influence of traditional banking systems.

As grassroots movements pushing for Bitcoin adoption gain traction, especially in hyperinflationary economies globally, the possibility of Bitcoin replacing traditional monetary systems becomes more credible and compelling. Bitcoin's unique ability to function independently from government control, along with its capacity to serve as a secure, inflation-resistant store of value, resonates strongly with those disillusioned by the shortcomings of fiat currencies. Predictions indicate that as awareness of Bitcoin's many benefits grows, it may not only act as a viable alternative investment but also become a foundational element of a new economic framework. This significant change could fundamentally alter how individuals engage with money daily, leading to an era where Bitcoin is seen not just as a digital asset but as a powerful indicator of the systemic issues in fiat currency and the potential for a more stable and resilient financial future for everyone.

Chapter 5: Bitcoin as an Inflation Hedge

The Unique Properties of Bitcoin: Scarcity, Security, and Decentralization

The properties of Bitcoin, particularly its scarcity and security, serve as foundational elements that distinctly set it apart from traditional fiat currencies. Scarcity stands out as one of Bitcoin's most defining characteristics, given that its total supply is capped at 21 million coins. This predetermined limit creates an intrinsic value, similar to that of precious metals like gold, which have historically been regarded as reliable stores of value over time. In contrast, fiat currencies can be printed at will by central banks, which often leads to inflation and a gradual erosion of purchasing power for consumers. As more investors and crypto enthusiasts actively seek alternatives to fiat money in the current economic landscape, a deeper understanding of Bitcoin's fixed supply becomes crucial in recognizing its potential role as a hedge against inflation and as a dependable store of value that can withstand the test of time.

'Security in Bitcoin encompasses a variety of critical aspects, including the integrity of the entire network and the effective safeguarding of individual assets held within it. The decentralized structure of Bitcoin's blockchain ensures that all transactions are recorded in a transparent and unchangeable manner, making it nearly impossible to alter transaction history without the consensus of the network participants. This high level of security stands in stark contrast to traditional fiat systems, where central authorities possess the power to manipulate currency values and engage in actions that can significantly erode public trust. For investors, the robust security offered by Bitcoin serves as a compelling argument for viewing it not merely as a speculative asset, but rather as a reliable and potentially stable investment in an increasingly unpredictable and volatile economic environment.'

The historical evolution of money underscores the profound significance of Bitcoin's distinctive properties. From the early days of barter systems to the use of gold, and now to the rise of digital currencies, each transformation has sought to address the inherent limitations of prior forms of money. While gold once stood as the universally accepted standard for wealth, it proved inadequate for facilitating transactions in an ever-evolving and increasingly digital world. Bitcoin emerges as a compelling solution to this pressing challenge, skillfully combining the scarcity associated with gold and the convenience offered by digital currencies. Investors who recognize and appreciate this evolutionary trajectory can gain deeper insights into why Bitcoin is steadily gaining traction as a credible alternative to traditional fiat currencies, particularly when considering the systemic flaws that are often inherent in the latter.

Central bank policies have significant and far-reaching implications for the value of fiat currencies, frequently resulting in inflationary pressures that substantially erode consumer purchasing power over time. As central banks increasingly engage in quantitative easing and implement various expansionary measures, the risk of hyperinflation emerges as a pressing concern for consumers and investors alike, generating anxiety about the stability of their financial futures. In this context, Bitcoin, with its carefully algorithmically controlled supply, presents a compelling counterbalance to these potentially destabilizing monetary policies. Real-world case studies from hyperinflationary economies, such as those seen in Venezuela and Zimbabwe, vividly illustrate how Bitcoin can serve as a safe haven for individuals seeking to preserve their wealth against the relentless devaluation of their local currencies. This critical aspect of Bitcoin's utility becomes particularly compelling for those navigating uncertain and turbulent economic climates, providing an alternative that empowers them to protect their financial well-being amidst widespread instability.

As grassroots movements advocating for Bitcoin adoption continue to grow and gain momentum, the psychological effects of fiat currency dependence on consumer behavior become increasingly apparent and significant. Many individuals have been conditioned to trust and rely on fiat money, often overlooking its inherent vulnerabilities and weaknesses. However, as awareness of Bitcoin's unique properties spreads and becomes more widespread, there is a notable shift in mindset toward valuing scarcity, security, and decentralization. This transformation in perception is not merely beneficial but essential for Bitcoin's potential to effectively replace traditional monetary systems that have long been in place. As investors and crypto enthusiasts engage with these revolutionary concepts and ideas, they play a vital and active role in shaping the future of money, a future that prioritizes stability, resilience, and independence over the unpredictable whims of central banks and traditional financial institutions.

'Real-World Case Studies of Bitcoin Utilization in Various Inflationary Contexts'

In examining the real-world applications of Bitcoin within various inflationary contexts, it becomes essential to thoroughly showcase how this innovative digital asset has emerged as a viable and increasingly popular alternative to failing fiat currencies. Numerous historical case studies reveal how countries that have experienced severe hyperinflation, such as Venezuela and Zimbabwe, turned to Bitcoin as a crucial means of preserving their wealth during tumultuous economic times. In these nations, where local currencies rapidly lost value and purchasing power dwindled, citizens began to embrace Bitcoin not only for its potential appreciation over time but also as a more stable medium of exchange, particularly when traditional financial systems and infrastructures collapsed. This significant transition illustrates the intrinsic properties of Bitcoin that empower individuals to effectively protect their purchasing power and financial stability in the face of widespread economic turmoil and uncertainty, highlighting its potential role as a safeguard against the failures of conventional currencies.

Venezuela serves as a striking and poignant example of Bitcoin's critical role during a period of extreme hyperinflation. As the country faced astronomical inflation rates, which reached over 1,000,000% in 2018, the national currency, the bolívar, became nearly worthless and lost its purchasing power almost entirely. In response to this dire situation, many Venezuelans turned to Bitcoin as a means to safeguard their savings and facilitate everyday transactions. Peer-to-peer trading platforms flourished and thrived, enabling individuals to buy and sell Bitcoin using local currencies or even goods and services. This grassroots movement not only provided an avenue for financial transactions but also demonstrated how Bitcoin could serve as a viable alternative financial system for those disenfranchised and marginalized by their government's ineffective monetary policies. In this way, it fostered a profound sense of financial autonomy and independence, allowing individuals to navigate and survive despite the dire economic conditions surrounding them.

Similarly, Zimbabwe's experience with hyperinflation in the late 2000s serves as another compelling case study illustrating the devastating effects of economic mismanagement. At its peak, Zimbabwe's inflation rate exceeded an astonishing 89.7 sextillion percent, rendering the Zimbabwean dollar virtually worthless and leading to widespread poverty and hardship. In this climate of extreme economic instability, Bitcoin emerged as a vital digital lifeline for many. The rise of cryptocurrency exchanges and the formation of local Bitcoin trading groups empowered Zimbabweans to bypass traditional banking systems, which were either completely non-functional or excessively regulated. The ability to transact in Bitcoin not only provided a more stable store of value amidst the chaos but also greatly facilitated international remittances. This innovative approach offered a crucial support mechanism for families grappling with the fallout of the economic crisis, allowing them to receive funds from abroad and maintain some semblance of financial stability during tumultuous times.

The analysis comparing Bitcoin to traditional investments during inflationary periods highlights Bitcoin's potential as an effective safeguard against the ongoing threat of currency devaluation. In a financial landscape where fiat currencies are heavily influenced by central bank policies and decisions, the limited supply of Bitcoin becomes particularly appealing to investors. Historical evidence demonstrates that during times of significant high inflation, conventional assets such as stocks and bonds frequently find themselves struggling to keep pace with the rapid decline in purchasing power. On the other hand, Bitcoin has consistently shown remarkable strength and substantial growth, thereby establishing itself as a more reliable store of value for investors who are looking to protect and preserve their wealth during times of economic instability and uncertainty.

The implications of these real-world case studies extend far beyond individual financial strategies; they significantly highlight the transformative potential of Bitcoin in reshaping entire monetary systems. As inflation continues to erode the value of fiat currencies worldwide at an alarming rate, the grassroots movements advocating for Bitcoin adoption in hyperinflationary economies signal a much broader shift towards decentralized finance and innovative financial solutions. These movements not only reflect the urgent need for robust alternatives to traditional monetary systems but also emphasize the critical importance of Bitcoin's underlying technology in fostering economic independence and resilience across various communities. As more individuals increasingly turn to Bitcoin to effectively navigate the complex challenges posed by fiat inflation, its role as a revolutionary financial instrument becomes increasingly evident and undeniable, cementing its place in the future of finance.

Comparative Performance Analysis: Bitcoin in Relation to Traditional Fiat Currencies

In the evolving landscape of modern finance, a thorough comparative performance analysis of Bitcoin and fiat currency reveals stark contrasts that underscore the limitations and vulnerabilities of traditional monetary systems. Fiat currencies, which are government-issued and not backed by any physical commodities, have been plagued by rampant inflation and significant devaluation, primarily due to excessive printing and manipulation of supply. This detrimental practice has systematically eroded purchasing power, leaving consumers increasingly vulnerable and often leading to severe economic crises. In stark contrast, Bitcoin, with its fixed supply cap of 21 million coins, presents a fundamentally different monetary model that inherently protects against inflationary pressures and fosters a more stable economic environment. This distinction highlights the potential of cryptocurrencies to offer a more resilient alternative to conventional financial systems.

The historical evolution of money vividly showcases a remarkable transition from tangible assets like gold to digital assets such as Bitcoin. For centuries, gold has served as a stable store of value, revered for its rarity and enduring worth. However, its physical limitations, including issues related to storage and transport, have rendered it less practical in today's rapid and highly interconnected economy. In response to these challenges, Bitcoin emerged as a revolutionary alternative, harnessing the power of blockchain technology to provide unparalleled decentralization and enhanced security. This significant transition represents not merely a change in the form of money, but also a profound shift in the foundational principles that govern it. This evolution emphasizes vital aspects such as scarcity, transparency, and accessibility, which fiat currencies have increasingly struggled to deliver effectively in modern financial systems.

Inflation is a critical factor that underscores the inherent shortcomings of fiat currencies. As central banks adopt aggressive monetary policies, such as extensive quantitative easing and persistently low-interest rates, the result is often a significant devaluation of currency that ultimately diminishes consumer purchasing power. This phenomenon has been extensively documented during various periods of economic distress, where fiat currencies have lost substantial value, while Bitcoin has demonstrated notable resilience and stability. Real-world case studies in hyperinflationary economies, such as Venezuela and Zimbabwe, vividly illustrate how Bitcoin has emerged as a viable hedge against the collapse of local fiat currencies. In these scenarios, individuals have turned to Bitcoin as a means to preserve their wealth in an increasingly unstable and unpredictable economic environment, enabling them to safeguard their financial futures amidst the turmoil.

Central bank policies play a crucial role in determining the value of fiat currencies, significantly influencing their stability and reliability. These monetary policies can lead to erratic fluctuations and a pervasive lack of confidence among consumers and investors alike. In contrast, Bitcoin operates independently of any central authority, providing a decentralized alternative that is inherently less susceptible to political and economic manipulation. During inflationary periods, traditional investments such as stocks and bonds often struggle to maintain their value and can experience significant losses, while Bitcoin has frequently outperformed these assets, attracting considerable interest from investors seeking refuge from the volatility induced by fiat currencies. This growing interest highlights the appeal of Bitcoin as a potential safe haven during times of economic uncertainty.

The growing grassroots movements advocating for Bitcoin adoption in economies grappling with hyperinflation further underscore its potential to serve as a viable replacement for traditional monetary systems. As individuals and communities become increasingly aware of the inherent flaws and limitations of fiat currencies, they are turning to Bitcoin as a compelling solution that offers both autonomy and enhanced security. This significant transition not only reflects a notable shift in consumer behavior but also indicates a broader and more widespread acceptance of digital currencies as a legitimate and viable form of money. As we look toward the future, the potential for Bitcoin to establish itself as a primary monetary standard becomes even more pronounced, actively challenging the very foundations of fiat currency and redefining what constitutes the essence of value within the global economy. This evolution in financial thinking could lead to transformative changes, allowing for a more decentralized and equitable economic landscape.

Chapter 6: The Role of Central Bank Policies and Their Significant Impact on the Economy

The Significance of Central Banks in Shaping Monetary Policy

Central banks play a crucial and multifaceted role in shaping monetary policy, which has a direct and significant impact on the value of fiat currencies and, consequently, the purchasing power of consumers in everyday transactions. By strategically manipulating interest rates and controlling the money supply, central banks aim to maintain overall economic stability and foster growth. However, their actions often lead to unintended consequences, such as inflation, which gradually erodes the value of money over time and diminishes its purchasing power. A thorough examination of the historical context of monetary policy reveals a recurring pattern of overreach, where excessive money printing in response to various economic crises has resulted in diminished trust and confidence in fiat currencies among the public. This persistent erosion of trust has sparked a growing interest in alternative forms of money, particularly Bitcoin, which presents a decentralized, inflation-resistant alternative that appeals to those seeking more reliable financial options in an uncertain economic landscape.

Historically, the evolution of money has transitioned from tangible assets, such as gold and silver, to fiat currencies that are primarily backed by government decree and trust. This significant shift has empowered central banks to exert a greater degree of control over the economy, allowing for more flexible monetary policy. However, this transition has also resulted in systemic vulnerabilities within the financial system. The practices of central banks, particularly their strategies of quantitative easing and maintaining low-interest rates during periods of economic downturns, have inadvertently contributed to the creation of asset bubbles and exacerbated wealth inequality among different segments of the population. As central banks continue to expand the money supply without a corresponding increase in economic growth, the risks of hyperinflation become more pronounced. This looming threat prompts individuals and investors alike to seek refuge in assets that possess intrinsic value, such as Bitcoin, which is increasingly viewed as a hedge against inflation and economic instability.

Inflation has emerged as a significant and pressing concern for consumers who increasingly witness their purchasing power steadily erode as fiat currency becomes less valuable over time. Central banks often downplay the detrimental effects of inflation, choosing instead to focus on short-term economic growth and stability. However, the stark reality is that prolonged periods of inflation can lead to a troubling cycle of dependence on fiat currency. In this environment, consumers feel an overwhelming pressure to spend their money quickly before it loses even more value. This scenario creates a fertile ground for the emergence and growth of alternative currencies like Bitcoin. Unlike fiat currency, Bitcoin and similar cryptocurrencies are designed to be deflationary and can effectively preserve purchasing power over time. This makes them an increasingly compelling choice for investors who are actively seeking stability and security in their financial assets.

Real-world case studies vividly illustrate Bitcoin's remarkable effectiveness as a hedge against inflation, particularly in countries grappling with severe hyperinflation. For instance, in nations like

Venezuela and Zimbabwe, citizens have increasingly turned to Bitcoin as a vital means of preserving their wealth when their national currencies have dramatically collapsed. These grassroots movements powerfully highlight the rising demand for a decentralized financial system that grants individuals greater autonomy and control over their wealth. The policies implemented by central banks, which frequently prioritize the interests of governments above those of consumers, have contributed to a growing sense of disillusionment with traditional fiat currencies. This discontent has further intensified the adoption of Bitcoin in regions severely affected by economic instability and currency devaluation.

The impact of central bank monetary policy extends far beyond the borders of individual nations; it profoundly influences global markets and shapes investment strategies on an international scale. During periods of rising inflation, Bitcoin has demonstrated remarkable resilience compared to traditional investments, frequently outperforming various asset classes such as stocks and bonds. As inflation steadily erodes the value of fiat currencies, a growing number of investors increasingly recognize Bitcoin's potential as a reliable store of value. The notable rise of Bitcoin, along with the expanding advocacy for its broader adoption, suggests a transformative shift in the monetary landscape. This shift reveals the significant limitations of fiat currency, while simultaneously allowing the promise of decentralized alternatives to gain substantial traction among consumers and investors alike, further highlighting the evolving nature of financial systems worldwide.

Quantitative Easing and Its Impact on the Value of Fiat Currency

Quantitative easing (QE) is a monetary policy strategy employed by central banks to stimulate economic growth by significantly increasing the money supply, primarily through the acquisition of government securities and financial assets. This practice has been extensively utilized in response to severe economic downturns and crises, such as the 2008 financial crisis and the recent COVID-19 pandemic. While the primary goal of QE is to lower interest rates, thereby encouraging lending and investment across various sectors, it also carries profound and far-reaching implications for the value of fiat currencies. As central banks inject an increasing amount of money into the economy, the resultant rise in money supply can lead to currency devaluation, which erodes consumers' purchasing power over time. This situation fosters an environment that is particularly conducive to inflationary pressures, further complicating the economic landscape and impacting everyday financial transactions for individuals and businesses alike.

The historical context of money powerfully illustrates how various monetary policies can significantly disrupt traditional systems of currency. From the gold standard to the emergence of fiat currencies, each evolution has been characterized by differing degrees of stability, trust, and public confidence. Fiat money, which is backed solely by government decree rather than any tangible assets, becomes particularly vulnerable to the detrimental effects of an excessive money supply. In the aftermath of quantitative easing, many investors have observed a troubling trend: as central banks generate vast amounts of currency, the intrinsic value of fiat money diminishes. This decline leads to a growing loss of confidence among consumers and investors alike, raising serious concerns about the long-term viability of such systems. This phenomenon has sparked a renewed interest in alternative monetary systems, particularly Bitcoin, which offers the advantages of a fixed supply and operates independently of the policies implemented by central banks. As such, Bitcoin is increasingly viewed as a potential hedge against the shortcomings of traditional fiat currencies.

Inflation, primarily driven by rampant money printing, poses significant challenges for consumers across various economic sectors. As prices continue to rise, the real value of wages stagnates or even declines, resulting in a decrease in overall purchasing power for the average individual and family. Historical data consistently show that periods of high inflation correlate with increased public discontent, social unrest, and economic instability. In this complex context, Bitcoin emerges as a potential safeguard against inflationary pressures that threaten financial stability. With its capped supply of 21 million coins, Bitcoin provides a stark contrast to the fluidity and unpredictability of fiat currencies, presenting itself as a viable and attractive store of value. Real-world case studies from various countries demonstrate that during inflationary episodes, Bitcoin often appreciates in value, making it an appealing option for investors seeking to preserve their wealth against the devaluation of traditional currencies and to mitigate the effects of inflation on their financial wellbeing.

Central bank policies, particularly those involving quantitative easing, exert profound and far-reaching effects on the valuation of fiat currencies. As these institutions adopt increasingly aggressive monetary measures, the resulting influx of capital into the economy can create significant asset bubbles, distort essential market signals, and ultimately lead to a misallocation of valuable resources. This destabilization often prompts investors to seek refuge in more resilient forms of currency, such as Bitcoin, which is perceived as a safer alternative during times of economic uncertainty. A comparative analysis of Bitcoin and traditional investments, particularly during inflationary periods, reveals that Bitcoin frequently outperforms stocks and bonds, making it an increasingly appealing option for those aiming to hedge against the unpredictability and inherent risks associated with fiat currency fluctuations.

In light of these profound challenges, grassroots movements advocating for Bitcoin adoption in hyperinflationary economies have gained significant momentum and visibility. Countries experiencing extreme inflation, such as Venezuela and Zimbabwe, vividly showcase the urgent and pressing need for alternative monetary solutions that can provide stability and security. Bitcoin's decentralized nature uniquely empowers individuals to bypass traditional banking systems, allowing them to retain and protect their wealth in the face of government-induced financial crises and instability. As awareness of Bitcoin's numerous advantages continues to grow among various populations, it is poised to play a crucial and transformative role in reshaping the future of finance. This positions Bitcoin as a viable alternative to fiat currencies, which are increasingly viewed as broken money that fails to serve the needs of the people. The ongoing trajectory of monetary policy and its direct impact on currency value will continue to influence investor behavior and sentiment, potentially accelerating Bitcoin's acceptance and recognition as a mainstream asset class in the global financial landscape.

Bitcoin's Reaction to Actions Taken by Central Banks

Bitcoin's response to central bank actions illustrates a unique and transformative shift in the landscape of monetary policy and economic stability that is noteworthy. Central banks have historically wielded significant power over fiat currencies, implementing various measures such as quantitative easing and interest rate adjustments to effectively manage economic fluctuations and maintain stability. However, these strategies often lead to unintended consequences, including rampant inflation, market distortions, and the erosion of purchasing power for consumers. In contrast, Bitcoin operates on a decentralized model that is immune to political manipulation and the whims of monetary policy, presenting itself as a robust and appealing alternative for investors seeking stability and security during turbulent economic times. This underlying structure allows Bitcoin to maintain its value more consistently than traditional fiat currencies, making it an increasingly attractive option for those wary of central bank interventions.

The historical evolution of money significantly underscores the necessity for alternative systems. From the gold standard to various fiat currencies, each monetary system has faced a unique set of challenges that have ultimately led to its decline over time. The transition from tangible assets like gold to fiat currencies marked a significant departure from intrinsic value, allowing governments to print money without any real restraint or accountability. This shift has resulted in the current predicament associated with fiat money, which is characterized by excessive supply and considerable inflationary pressures that devalue currency. In stark contrast, Bitcoin, with its capped supply of 21 million coins, presents a unique alternative by offering a deflationary asset that has the potential to preserve value over time and resist the pitfalls of traditional monetary systems.

Inflation, which is a direct consequence of the actions taken by central banks, has a profound and often detrimental impact on consumers' purchasing power. As fiat currencies steadily lose their value over time, the overall cost of goods and services continues to rise, effectively diminishing the wealth of individuals who rely on these currencies for their daily transactions and savings. In contrast, Bitcoin is uniquely designed as a scarce digital asset, positioning it as a compelling hedge against inflationary pressures. Numerous real-world case studies have illustrated its remarkable ability to retain value even in hyperinflationary environments. For example, in countries grappling with severe economic turmoil, such as Venezuela and Zimbabwe, Bitcoin has emerged as a crucial lifeline. It enables individuals to protect their wealth and engage in commerce without being hindered by the limitations and instability of a failing national currency. In these scenarios, Bitcoin has proven essential for many seeking financial stability amidst chaos.

Central bank policies play a crucial role in directly influencing the value of fiat currencies, often leading to increased volatility and uncertainty in traditional investment markets. During inflationary periods, assets such as stocks and bonds frequently experience declines as rising interest rates tend to hinder overall economic growth and investor confidence. In contrast, Bitcoin, with its unique attributes and decentralized nature, has the potential to thrive in these challenging environments. A comparative analysis illustrates that Bitcoin has consistently outperformed many traditional investments during significant inflationary episodes, further reinforcing its emerging role as a viable asset class for investors who are seeking to diversify their portfolios and effectively mitigate risk in an unpredictable economic landscape.

The rise of Bitcoin is not solely a reaction to the actions taken by central banks; it also embodies the spirit of grassroots movements that fervently advocate for its adoption in economies struggling with the severe consequences of hyperinflation. This phenomenon underscores the increasing recognition of Bitcoin as a viable solution to the myriad problems tied to an over-reliance on fiat currency. As individuals and communities around the world increasingly strive for financial independence through the use of Bitcoin, it becomes increasingly evident that its foundational technology—blockchain, coupled with decentralization—presents a promising path toward establishing a more stable and resilient monetary future. Looking ahead into the coming years, the potential for Bitcoin to effectively replace traditional monetary systems appears quite promising, particularly as awareness of its numerous benefits continues to grow among investors, crypto enthusiasts, and the general public alike.

Chapter 7: Comparative Analysis of Investments

Conventional Investments During Times of Inflationary Economic Conditions

Traditional investments have long been regarded as reliable avenues for wealth preservation, especially during inflationary periods when the purchasing power of fiat currencies is eroded. Historically, assets such as real estate, commodities, and stocks have been preferred by investors who are seeking to mitigate the adverse effects of rising prices and protect their financial assets. However, as inflation increasingly stems from unsustainable fiscal policies and excessive government spending, the effectiveness of these traditional investment strategies is coming under scrutiny. With the overprinting of money and the consequent devaluation of fiat currencies, many investors are now finding themselves reassessing the long-term viability of conventional assets as effective hedges against inflation, questioning whether these time-honored approaches can still safeguard their wealth in a rapidly changing economic landscape.

Real estate has often been viewed as a reliable safe haven during periods of inflation, as property values generally tend to rise in line with or even above the rate of inflation over time. However, the market is not without its numerous pitfalls and challenges. For instance, high interest rates can significantly dampen housing demand, making it more difficult for potential buyers to secure financing. Additionally, the increased costs of materials can adversely affect both construction and renovation projects, leading to delays and budget overruns. Furthermore, the cyclical nature of real estate markets means that they can undergo substantial downturns, which can leave investors vulnerable to financial losses. While historical trends indicate that real estate can provide some level of protection against inflation, it is crucial to recognize that it is not immune to the same economic forces that drive the depreciation of fiat currency. Investors should proceed with caution and remain aware of the inherent risks involved in the real estate market.

Commodities, particularly precious metals such as gold, have long been regarded as a reliable hedge against inflation. The intrinsic value of gold, coupled with its limited supply, positions it as an attractive alternative to fiat currency, especially in times of economic uncertainty and financial instability. However, the performance of gold can often be inconsistent, subject to various influences such as geopolitical events, economic data releases, and shifts in investor sentiment. While gold is frequently promoted as a secure store of value, its inherent volatility, along with the practical challenges associated with ownership, custody, and storage, may prompt some investors to rethink its role in their investment portfolios during periods of rising inflation.

Stocks are generally viewed as a long-term growth investment, but they can also be significantly affected by inflationary pressures. As costs rise, companies may opt to pass these increases on to consumers, which could potentially lead to higher revenues and profits for those businesses. However, inflation also has the potential to compress profit margins and diminish consumer purchasing power, creating a complex and often contradictory relationship between stock performance and inflation trends. Additionally, the heavy reliance on monetary policy, such as maintaining low interest rates to stimulate economic growth, can lead to the formation of market bubbles that may eventually burst when the economic environment changes. Therefore, while equities can offer some degree of protection against inflation, they are certainly not a foolproof or guaranteed solution for investors looking to safeguard their portfolios.

In contrast, Bitcoin presents a compelling and unique alternative to traditional investments, especially during periods of inflation. As a decentralized digital currency with a capped supply, Bitcoin is specifically engineered to resist the inflationary pressures that often plague fiat currencies. Real-world case studies from hyperinflationary economies have effectively demonstrated Bitcoin's remarkable ability to maintain its value when traditional assets falter and lose purchasing power. Furthermore, Bitcoin's increasing adoption and integration into the broader financial ecosystem suggest that it may serve as a more effective hedge against inflation compared to conventional assets. As investors and crypto enthusiasts delve deeper into the evolving landscape of money and finance, understanding Bitcoin's pivotal role in this context can provide invaluable insights into securing and preserving wealth in an inflationary environment. This understanding can empower investors to make informed decisions, potentially leading to more stable financial futures.

Bitcoin Compared to Stocks and Bonds: An Analysis of History

Bitcoin and traditional financial instruments such as stocks and bonds have coexisted within a complex and often dynamic economic landscape, with each influenced by historical shifts in monetary policy, regulatory changes, and evolving investor sentiment. While stocks and bonds have long been regarded as the foundational cornerstones of diverse investment portfolios, their performance is frequently tied to the stability of fiat currencies, which are inherently susceptible to inflationary pressures and the varying interventions of central banks. In stark contrast, Bitcoin emerged in the wake of the 2008 financial crisis, presenting itself as a decentralized digital asset specifically designed to operate independently of the conventional financial system. This subchapter delves into the historical perspectives and key developments that shape the ongoing debate between Bitcoin and conventional investments, highlighting the fundamental differences and potential implications for investors in today's market.

The historical evolution of money reveals a gradual and fascinating transition from tangible assets such as gold, which have been revered for centuries, to the more abstract realm of fiat currencies, and now, we are witnessing the rise of digital currencies like Bitcoin. Gold has always been valued for its scarcity, intrinsic qualities, and the trust people have placed in it, serving as a reliable and stable store of value across various civilizations. However, with the introduction of fiat money—currencies that are backed not by physical commodities but by government decree—societies have encountered systemic issues. These include rampant inflation fueled by excessive printing and poor fiscal governance, leading to significant economic instability. The lessons learned from the historical failures and shortcomings of fiat currencies underscore the potential of Bitcoin and similar digital currencies as a return to sound money principles. In this new paradigm, supply is not only limited but also predictable, which could pave the way for a more stable and resilient financial future.

Inflation and the erosion of purchasing power have increasingly become defining characteristics of fiat currency systems, especially in the context of expansive monetary policies implemented by central banks. As these institutions respond to economic downturns with aggressive stimulus measures aimed at revitalizing growth, the resulting increase in the money supply often leads to inflationary pressures that significantly diminish consumers' purchasing power over time. In stark contrast, Bitcoin's fixed supply of 21 million coins introduces a deflationary aspect that positions it as a robust hedge against inflation. Numerous real-world case studies from hyperinflationary economies around the globe illustrate how individuals have turned to Bitcoin as a critical lifeline, effectively preserving their wealth and financial stability when traditional currencies fail to maintain their value and purchasing power.

Central bank policies have a profound and significant impact on the value of fiat currencies, often leading to a cyclical pattern of boom and bust that greatly affects both stock and bond markets. The intricate relationship between monetary policy and asset performance becomes particularly evident during periods of inflation, where the purchasing power of fiat currencies consistently declines. This decline results in increased uncertainties regarding stock valuations and bond yields, creating a volatile investment environment. In these challenging contexts, Bitcoin has emerged as a compelling alternative investment that not only retains its value but also tends to thrive when traditional markets face significant struggles. Numerous comparative analyses frequently demonstrate that Bitcoin has the potential to outperform stocks and bonds during inflationary crises, thereby attracting a growing number of investors who are actively seeking refuge from the depreciation of fiat currencies. As a result, Bitcoin's appeal continues to rise as a hedge against economic instability.

Grassroots movements advocating for Bitcoin adoption in economies suffering from hyperinflation reflect a growing recognition of its utility as a revolutionary new form of money that challenges established norms. The psychological effects of fiat currency dependence have conditioned consumers to accept inflation as an inevitable aspect of economic life, often leading to a sense of helplessness. However, as awareness of Bitcoin's numerous advantages spreads, individuals are beginning to embrace its significant potential to disrupt the status quo and empower them financially. The technology behind Bitcoin, which is grounded in blockchain and decentralization, offers a transparent and secure means of conducting transactions. This transparency and security further entice those who are increasingly disillusioned with the traditional financial system and its shortcomings. As we look to the future, the potential of Bitcoin to not only complement but potentially replace traditional monetary systems becomes a compelling narrative for investors, crypto enthusiasts, and everyday individuals alike, igniting a movement that could reshape our economic landscape.

Diversification Strategies in an Inflationary Era

In an inflationary era, investors must adopt robust diversification strategies that not only protect their portfolios but also allow them to capitalize on emerging opportunities in a changing economic landscape. Traditional assets such as stocks and bonds frequently suffer during periods of high inflation, as rising prices erode purchasing power and significantly diminish investment returns over time. Consequently, investors are increasingly turning to alternative assets like Bitcoin and other cryptocurrencies, which have the potential to act as an effective hedge against inflation. By diversifying into cryptocurrencies and other non-correlated assets, investors can better mitigate the risks associated with fiat currency depreciation while simultaneously positioning themselves for sustainable long-term growth and financial stability in the face of economic uncertainties.

One effective strategy that many investors are considering is to allocate a significant portion of their investment portfolio to Bitcoin and other cryptocurrencies. This approach is rooted in the understanding that Bitcoin operates outside the traditional fiat monetary system, which has been plagued by excessive money printing, consistent devaluation, and systemic instability. Historically, during various inflationary episodes, Bitcoin has demonstrated remarkable resilience and even appreciation, making it an increasingly attractive option for those who are seeking to preserve and grow their wealth over time. By thoughtfully incorporating Bitcoin into their broader asset allocation strategy, investors can potentially safeguard their purchasing power against the relentless erosion and diminishing value caused by fiat inflation, thus enhancing their overall financial security in an unpredictable economic landscape.

In addition to exploring cryptocurrencies, investors should seriously consider diversifying their portfolios to include commodities, with a particular emphasis on precious metals such as gold and silver. Historically, these tangible assets have proven to be reliable safe havens during times of economic uncertainty and rising inflation. As fiat currencies experience depreciation and lose their purchasing power, tangible assets like gold and silver tend to maintain their intrinsic value, effectively providing a strong buffer against inflationary pressures. A well-rounded investment portfolio that incorporates both cutting-edge digital assets and traditional physical commodities can offer a more comprehensive and resilient defense against the negative impacts of central bank policies, which often lead to currency devaluation and economic instability. This strategic combination can help investors navigate the complexities of today's financial landscape more effectively.

Another diversification strategy that many investors consider involves exploring real estate investments, which can provide a robust hedge against inflation, as property values often rise in tandem with increasing costs of living over time. Real estate offers the dual benefits of capital appreciation and rental income, making it a compelling and attractive option for investors who are actively looking to enhance and diversify their portfolios. By investing in various types of properties or real estate investment trusts (REITs), individuals can benefit from the tangible asset's significant potential to outpace inflation while simultaneously generating consistent passive income streams that can provide financial stability. This makes real estate a particularly appealing choice for those seeking long-term growth and security in their investment strategies.

Finally, investors should remain open to exploring not only emerging technologies but also sectors that tend to thrive in an inflationary environment. Industries such as renewable energy, healthcare, and technology-driven innovations frequently demonstrate resilience amid economic turmoil and uncertainty. By diversifying their portfolios into these sectors, investors can effectively capture growth opportunities that align with the broader shifts in market dynamics and economic trends. Ultimately, a well-considered diversification strategy that includes Bitcoin, various commodities, real estate, and innovative sectors can provide a comprehensive and robust approach to navigating the challenges posed by inflationary pressures and the inherent weaknesses of fiat currency systems. This multifaceted strategy can enhance financial stability and potential returns in a fluctuating economic landscape.

Chapter 8: Monetary Policy and Economic Crises

'The Connection Between Monetary Policy and Economic Recessions'

Monetary policy plays a crucial role in shaping the economic landscape, significantly determining the overall health and stability of a nation's economy. Central banks, which are tasked with maintaining economic stability and promoting sustainable growth, utilize a variety of tools and strategies to influence interest rates, regulate money supply, and control inflation. However, an over-reliance on these monetary policies can lead to detrimental effects, particularly during times of economic downturns and crises. When central banks engage in extensive money printing to stimulate growth or mitigate the impacts of financial crises, the result is often rampant inflation, which erodes purchasing power and creates a troubling cycle of dependency on fiat currency. This recurring pattern underscores the inherent vulnerabilities present in fiat money systems, which can be further exacerbated by aggressive monetary interventions that fail to adequately address the underlying economic issues and structural problems that contribute to economic instability.

Historically, the link between monetary policy and economic downturns reveals a clear and concerning pattern where expansive monetary policies contribute significantly to financial instability. For instance, the 2008 financial crisis was fueled by an environment of excessive lending combined with a dramatic increase in the money supply, which led to the formation of asset bubbles and subsequent market collapses. Investors and crypto enthusiasts can draw compelling parallels to more recent events, where central banks responded to economic shocks with unprecedented monetary measures that have reshaped the financial landscape. The result of these actions has often been a pronounced devaluation of currency and a growing loss of trust in traditional financial systems, which has subsequently sparked a greater interest in alternative forms of money. This interest has particularly focused on Bitcoin, which offers a decentralized solution that operates outside the control of central banks, providing an appealing alternative for those seeking stability and independence from conventional monetary systems.

As inflation continues to erode the value of fiat currency, consumers increasingly find their purchasing power diminishing, which leads to heightened economic distress for many households and individuals. This troubling scenario paints a grim picture for those who are relying on fiat money as a reliable store of value in uncertain times. In stark contrast, Bitcoin presents a highly appealing hedge against inflation, with its supply strictly capped at 21 million coins, ensuring scarcity. As more investors turn to Bitcoin during periods of economic uncertainty and instability, real-world case studies increasingly demonstrate its resilience when compared to traditional investments. For instance, during various inflationary periods, Bitcoin has often outperformed stocks and bonds, showcasing its potential as a robust safeguard for wealth as fiat currencies falter and lose their purchasing power. This trend suggests that Bitcoin may not only serve as an alternative investment but also as a vital component of a diversified portfolio aimed at preserving financial stability in turbulent economic climates.

Central bank policies not only impact the immediate value of fiat currencies but also play a crucial role in shaping long-term investor sentiment across various markets. The unpredictable nature of monetary interventions can lead to significant market volatility, prompting many investors to seek stability in alternative assets. This noticeable shift towards Bitcoin reflects a growing awareness of the inherent limitations of traditional fiat systems and a strong desire for greater financial autonomy among individuals. Investors are increasingly recognizing that Bitcoin's decentralized nature, which is firmly underpinned by blockchain technology, offers not just a safe haven from inflationary pressures but also a viable pathway toward a more equitable financial future. This future holds the promise of being free from the unpredictable whims and policies of central banks, thereby empowering individuals and fostering a more resilient economic landscape.

The rise of grassroots movements advocating for Bitcoin adoption in hyperinflationary economies compellingly illustrates the profound connection between the failures of monetary policy and the urgent search for alternative currencies. As individuals confront the harsh and often devastating realities of depreciating fiat currencies, they are increasingly turning to Bitcoin not only as a means of preserving their wealth in the face of economic instability but also as a powerful tool for personal empowerment and financial autonomy. The psychological effects of a deep dependence on fiat currency can lead to a pervasive sense of helplessness and vulnerability among consumers, whereas Bitcoin actively fosters a renewed sense of agency and control over one's financial destiny. As we look toward the future, the potential for Bitcoin to disrupt and ultimately replace traditional monetary systems becomes increasingly plausible and compelling, especially as the persistent failures of fiat currencies become ever more evident, creating a fertile ground for the growth and acceptance of decentralized financial solutions that empower individuals globally.

Case Studies: Past Crises and Their Outcomes

In examining past financial crises, it is essential to highlight the significant outcomes that have profoundly shaped public perception and influenced economic policies concerning fiat currencies. One particularly notable case is the hyperinflation experienced in Zimbabwe during the late 2000s, where the government resorted to printing money indiscriminately in a desperate attempt to alleviate mounting economic challenges. The result of these actions was catastrophic, with inflation rates skyrocketing to an astronomical 89.7 sextillion percent in November 2008. This extreme situation rendered the Zimbabwean dollar practically worthless and led to widespread poverty, economic destabilization, and social unrest. As a direct consequence of these dire circumstances, many Zimbabweans sought refuge in alternative currencies, including the U.S. dollar and, more recently, Bitcoin, as viable means of preserving their value and conducting everyday transactions in a more stable manner.

Another significant example is the Weimar Republic in Germany after World War I, which experienced profound economic turmoil. The reparations imposed on Germany created an environment of financial instability, leading to massive money printing by the government as a means to meet its obligations. This reckless monetary policy spiraled into hyperinflation between 1921 and 1923, causing catastrophic effects on the economy. At its peak, prices doubled approximately every three days, creating a situation where citizens were forced to carry wheelbarrows full of cash just to purchase basic goods like bread or milk. The Weimar experience vividly illustrates how excessive fiat currency issuance can obliterate purchasing power and undermine trust in the monetary system, prompting individuals to seek more stable forms of money, such as commodities or foreign currencies. This historical precedent has significantly influenced contemporary discussions about Bitcoin, as many view it as a potential safeguard against similar monetary mismanagement and inflationary crises in today's economy.

The economic crisis of 2008 serves as a significant lens through which one can scrutinize the failures and limitations inherent in fiat currencies. This crisis, ignited by the subprime mortgage disaster, set off a chain reaction that resulted in a financial meltdown of unprecedented proportions. In response, central banks around the world implemented extraordinary measures, including extensive quantitative easing and the establishment of near-zero interest rates. While these interventions provided a temporary stabilization of financial markets, they simultaneously raised serious and long-term concerns regarding inflation and the devaluation of currencies. In the aftermath of this crisis, Bitcoin emerged as a groundbreaking alternative, capturing the attention of those who felt disillusioned and disenfranchised by conventional financial systems. With its fixed supply of 21 million coins, Bitcoin stands in stark contrast to the virtually limitless nature of fiat money, effectively positioning itself as a potential safeguard against the inflationary policies that have come to characterize the economic landscape following the events of 2008.

Furthermore, the ongoing economic turmoil in Venezuela provides a compelling and contemporary case study of hyperinflation and the pivotal role of alternative currencies in such a crisis. The

Venezuelan bolívar has experienced extreme and rapid devaluation due to a series of government policies that have exacerbated the situation, resulting in annual inflation rates surpassing an astonishing 1,000,000 percent. In this dire economic environment, citizens have increasingly turned to Bitcoin and various other cryptocurrencies as a viable means of escaping the collapsing economy and protecting their wealth. Grassroots movements advocating for the adoption of Bitcoin have gained significant momentum, effectively showcasing the digital currency's utility as a reliable store of value in an increasingly hyperinflationary setting. This notable shift not only highlights the profound failings of fiat currencies in such extreme circumstances but also underscores Bitcoin's potential to empower individuals who are facing severe economic oppression and instability in their daily lives.

In summary, these historical case studies provide a compelling examination of the vulnerabilities inherent in fiat monetary systems, particularly when they are subjected to mismanagement and excessive inflation. For investors and crypto enthusiasts alike, gaining a thorough understanding of these historical precedents is crucial in recognizing and appreciating Bitcoin's growing significance in the modern financial landscape. The comparative analysis of Bitcoin against traditional investments during these inflationary periods reveals a rapidly growing consensus that Bitcoin may indeed serve as a viable alternative, offering not only stability but also a robust hedge against the depreciating value of fiat currencies. This deepened understanding and awareness paves the way for broader acceptance and adoption of Bitcoin as we collectively move towards an increasingly uncertain economic future, where innovative financial solutions may become essential.

The Rise of Bitcoin as a Response to Policy Failures

The emergence of Bitcoin can be traced back to a widespread disillusionment with fiat currencies, especially in the wake of significant financial crises and rampant inflation that affected economies globally. As governments and central banks resorted to excessive money printing as a means to address persistent economic downturns, the purchasing power of traditional currencies diminished significantly, leading to a loss of trust among the populace. This policy failure not only highlighted the inherent weaknesses and vulnerabilities of fiat systems but also sparked a growing interest in alternative forms of money, with Bitcoin emerging at the forefront of this movement. Investors and crypto enthusiasts increasingly recognized Bitcoin as a viable solution to the numerous problems created by unsound monetary policies, positioning it as a revolutionary digital asset that could retain value over time and serve as a hedge against inflation and currency devaluation.

Historically, money has undergone significant evolution, transitioning from tangible assets such as gold to the emergence of decentralized digital currencies. This transition reflects society's ongoing quest for a dependable store of value and an efficient medium of exchange. Gold, which has long been revered for its scarcity and intrinsic value, has faced considerable challenges concerning its portability and divisibility in everyday transactions. In contrast, Bitcoin presents a modern digital alternative that is not only easily transferable and divisible but also maintains its scarcity through a capped supply of 21 million coins. This evolution represents a crucial response to the inadequacies often found in fiat systems, which can frequently be manipulated by governments to achieve short-term objectives, often at the expense of long-term economic stability and health. As such, the shift towards digital currencies highlights the desire for a more resilient and reliable financial system that aligns with contemporary economic needs.

The failures of fiat currency become particularly evident during inflationary periods, when consumers experience a significant erosion of their purchasing power due to continually rising prices. Central banks, in their attempts to stimulate economic growth and maintain stability, often end up exacerbating inflation through the implementation of loose monetary policies. This ongoing scenario has prompted a growing number of individuals and investors to rethink their investment strategies, actively seeking out alternative assets that can serve as a protective buffer against the devaluation of currency. In this context, Bitcoin has emerged as a particularly compelling option, bolstered by numerous real-world case studies that demonstrate its effectiveness as a hedge against inflation. In countries grappling with hyperinflation, we have witnessed citizens increasingly turning to Bitcoin as a means to preserve their wealth during tumultuous economic times, illustrating its potential utility and resilience in periods of economic distress and uncertainty.

Central bank policies play a significant and influential role in determining the value of fiat currencies, often leading to unpredictable fluctuations that can severely undermine consumer confidence in the financial system. As these institutions engage in various practices, such as quantitative easing and adjustments to interest rates, the consequences ripple throughout the economy, making it increasingly challenging for individuals and businesses to navigate financial stability. In stark contrast, Bitcoin operates entirely outside the control of any central authority, offering a decentralized alternative that is not subject to arbitrary policy changes or sudden regulatory shifts. This independence from traditional monetary systems significantly enhances Bitcoin's appeal, particularly among investors and individuals who prioritize stability, transparency, and long-term growth in their financial strategies.

The rise of grassroots movements advocating for Bitcoin adoption in hyperinflationary economies further underscores its immense potential to challenge and disrupt existing monetary systems. As individuals and communities increasingly seek viable solutions to the adverse effects caused by fiat currency dependence, Bitcoin emerges as a compelling pathway toward achieving financial sovereignty and independence. A deeper understanding of the technology behind Bitcoin, particularly blockchain and its inherently decentralized nature, empowers both investors and crypto enthusiasts alike to engage with this innovative financial instrument with greater confidence and clarity. As the world grapples with the far-reaching implications of fiat currency failures and the instability they bring, Bitcoin stands poised not only as a valuable asset but also as a transformative force that could redefine the future landscape of money itself.

Chapter 9: Grassroots Movements for Bitcoin Adoption

The Importance of Community in the Expansion of Bitcoin

The role of community in Bitcoin's growth truly cannot be overstated. Since its inception, Bitcoin has relied profoundly on a passionate and dedicated community of supporters who have tirelessly championed its numerous benefits over traditional fiat currencies. This grassroots support has proven instrumental in promoting awareness and fostering a deeper understanding of Bitcoin as a viable alternative in a world often plagued by the numerous pitfalls and challenges of fiat money. The community has not only encouraged dialogue but has actively fostered a rich culture of education, motivating potential investors and enthusiastic individuals to delve deeper into the complex implications of inflationary fiat systems. This includes exploring the historical evolution of money, tracing its journey from tangible assets like gold to the modern realm of digital currencies, thus enriching the overall discourse surrounding the future of financial systems.

As Bitcoin gained significant traction over the years, so too did the networks of exchanges, wallets, and platforms that facilitate its widespread use and adoption. These platforms are often community-driven, fostering a strong sense of shared purpose and collective identity among users. Enthusiasts frequently engage in vibrant discussions about the intricate technology that underpins Bitcoin, placing a strong emphasis on the critical importance of blockchain technology and the principles of decentralization. This collaborative spirit within the community has led to a dynamic environment where knowledge is not only shared but also where innovative ideas are rapidly adopted and implemented. Such active community engagement is vital for Bitcoin's resilience against various central bank policies that may undermine fiat currencies. It reinforces the widespread belief that a decentralized monetary system can not only survive but thrive outside the control and influence of traditional financial institutions, thereby promoting a more equitable financial landscape for all.

The community has also played an essential role in advocating for Bitcoin as a robust hedge against inflation. Numerous real-world case studies from hyperinflationary economies vividly illustrate how Bitcoin has provided a crucial alternative means of preserving value when local currencies fail to maintain their worth. In countries where citizens have faced the alarming erosion of their purchasing power over time, Bitcoin has emerged as a vital lifeline, enabling individuals to safeguard their assets from the detrimental consequences of reckless and unpredictable monetary policies. The collective experiences of these communities have further energized the narrative that Bitcoin is not merely a digital asset, but rather a revolutionary monetary solution that can empower consumers and offer them protection from the arbitrary whims of central authorities and financial systems. This evolution underscores Bitcoin's potential to reshape the future of finance and enhance economic resilience for people around the globe.

The psychological impact of relying on fiat currency has led a significant number of individuals to turn to Bitcoin as a compelling solution for their financial worries. A growing collective recognition of the harmful effects of inflation, coupled with the persistent loss of value in fiat currencies, has created a robust psychological resistance to the conventional financial system. This notable change in perspective has motivated an increasing number of people to consider Bitcoin not just as a currency, but as an effective means of preserving wealth, thereby reinforcing its role as a viable investment, especially during challenging times of inflation. Furthermore, the community's proactive initiatives to raise awareness about these pressing challenges have played a crucial role in establishing Bitcoin's credibility, legitimacy, and acceptance as a credible alternative store of value in the modern financial landscape.

Looking to the future, the community's influence on Bitcoin's trajectory remains not just pivotal but increasingly critical. As more individuals come to recognize the inherent limitations of fiat money and the pressing necessity for a decentralized alternative, the grassroots movements advocating for Bitcoin adoption will likely continue to expand at an impressive rate. These movements not only serve to educate others about the benefits of digital currency but also actively promote the compelling idea that Bitcoin has the potential to effectively replace traditional monetary systems. The ongoing and vibrant dialogue within the community regarding the role of monetary policy in addressing economic crises underscores a collective aspiration for a more equitable and just financial landscape. This discussion sets the stage for Bitcoin's continued growth and widespread acceptance in a world that is becoming increasingly disillusioned with fiat currencies and seeks innovative solutions to longstanding financial issues.

Case Studies of Hyperinflationary Economies

Case studies of hyperinflationary economies provide crucial insights into the systemic failures and pitfalls of fiat currency systems while also highlighting the potential of Bitcoin as a more stable alternative. Historical examples such as Zimbabwe in the late 2000s and Venezuela in recent years vividly illustrate how reckless money printing and severe mismanagement by central banks can culminate in catastrophic economic conditions that devastate the populace. In Zimbabwe, the government engaged in the reckless practice of printing vast amounts of currency to finance its burgeoning budget deficit, resulting in an astronomical inflation rate that shockingly peaked at 89.7 sextillion percent on a month-over-month basis. This extreme hyperinflation rendered the Zimbabwean dollar practically worthless, compelling citizens to resort to barter systems and the use of foreign currencies, including the US dollar, for everyday transactions and basic economic activities.

Similarly, Venezuela has faced one of the most severe hyperinflations ever recorded in history, a situation driven by a complex interplay of factors including significant political instability, plummeting oil prices, and rampant money printing by the government. As inflation skyrocketed, the bolívar dramatically lost its purchasing power, resulting in widespread shortages of essential goods and services that many citizens relied upon for their daily lives. The ongoing economic crisis prompted a significant number of Venezuelans to seek refuge in alternative currencies, including Bitcoin and other cryptocurrencies, as a means of safeguarding their wealth and facilitating necessary transactions in an increasingly unstable economic environment. This notable shift highlights the inherent vulnerabilities present in fiat currency systems, where the value of the currency itself is often subject to the unpredictable nature of policy decisions and the consequences of economic mismanagement.

These case studies reveal a significant and recurring theme: the failure of fiat currencies during periods of hyperinflation frequently prompts a desperate search for viable alternatives that can effectively maintain value while facilitating trade. In this context, Bitcoin, characterized by its fixed supply and decentralized nature, stands out as a particularly compelling option for individuals navigating hyperinflationary environments. The real-world adoption of Bitcoin in countries such as Venezuela vividly illustrates its potential not only as a reliable store of value but also as an effective medium of exchange, offering individuals a crucial means to circumvent the severe limitations imposed by their national currency. This transition towards cryptocurrency highlights a broader shift in how people seek financial stability amidst economic turmoil.

The impact of central bank policies on the value of fiat currency is an essential and multifaceted factor in the complex dynamics of hyperinflation. Central banks frequently resort to measures such as quantitative easing and other forms of expansionary monetary policies during periods of significant economic distress. These actions can contribute to a substantial devaluation of the currency over time. As citizens gradually lose faith in the stability of their currency, they often begin to seek out alternatives, which drives an increasing demand for assets like Bitcoin and other cryptocurrencies. This notable shift not only highlights the inherent shortcomings of fiat monetary systems but also emphasizes the growing recognition of Bitcoin as a viable hedge against inflation and a potential store of value in uncertain economic times.

In conclusion, the experiences of hyperinflationary economies serve as a stark reminder of the inherent vulnerabilities of fiat currencies and highlight the pressing need for alternative monetary systems that can withstand economic turmoil. Bitcoin's emergence as a viable option in these challenging contexts illustrates its significant potential to disrupt traditional finance and offer a more stable means of preserving value over time. As an increasing number of individuals and communities turn to Bitcoin in response to the devastating effects of hyperinflation, the case against fiat currencies becomes even more compelling. This trend reinforces the argument for a necessary shift towards decentralized forms of money that prioritize stability, resilience, and individual empowerment, paving the way for a more secure financial future.

Advocacy and Education: Spreading the Message

Advocacy and education play crucial roles in spreading awareness about the inherent flaws of fiat currency and the substantial advantages of adopting Bitcoin as an alternative financial system. As inflation rates continue to soar due to excessive money printing and the devaluation of fiat money, it becomes increasingly essential to inform both new and seasoned investors about the historical evolution of money, particularly the significant transition from gold to Bitcoin. This in-depth understanding fosters a deeper appreciation of Bitcoin as a viable alternative that not only preserves purchasing power effectively but also demonstrates resilience against the systemic failures that often plague traditional financial systems. By highlighting the rich historical context surrounding currency evolution, advocates can effectively communicate to a broader audience why Bitcoin is not merely a speculative asset but rather a necessary and innovative evolution in the landscape of monetary systems. This knowledge empowers individuals to make informed decisions about their financial futures and encourages greater participation in the cryptocurrency ecosystem.

Inflation remains a significant concern for consumers who depend on fiat currencies, which have repeatedly demonstrated an inability to maintain purchasing power over time. The continuous and often unchecked printing of money has resulted in diminishing returns for everyday consumers, leading to a gradual erosion of the value of their hard-earned savings. To address this pressing issue, educational initiatives that focus on real-world case studies illustrating the impact of inflation are crucial for both investors and crypto enthusiasts. These detailed case studies can effectively reveal how extreme hyperinflation in countries such as Venezuela and Zimbabwe has compelled citizens to explore alternatives like Bitcoin. This trend showcases Bitcoin's growing potential as a reliable hedge against the substantial loss of value that is often associated with fiat currency, highlighting the urgent need for individuals to consider alternative financial solutions in today's economic landscape.

The impact of central bank policies on the value of fiat currency is far-reaching and cannot be overstated. Central banks wield considerable control over monetary policy, which often leads to decisions that can trigger economic crises and exacerbate inflation. By taking the initiative to educate the public about how these monetary policies directly affect their financial well-being, advocates can effectively frame Bitcoin not merely as a speculative investment opportunity but as a proactive response to the mismanagement often seen in central banking practices. This deeper understanding empowers individuals to fully recognize the critical importance of decentralization in today's financial landscape and highlights the pivotal role that Bitcoin plays in helping reclaim financial autonomy and independence from traditional banking systems.

Moreover, grassroots movements advocating for Bitcoin adoption in hyperinflationary economies serve as compelling and powerful examples of Bitcoin's transformative potential in the financial landscape. As communities increasingly turn to Bitcoin as a means of achieving economic stability and security, these movements vividly illustrate the profound social and economic implications that accompany the adoption of a decentralized currency. By thoroughly highlighting these inspiring success stories and case studies, advocates can effectively motivate and inspire others to explore and consider Bitcoin as a viable solution to their own pressing financial struggles. This, in turn, fosters a more robust collective movement towards the widespread acceptance and practical use of Bitcoin as a legitimate alternative to traditional financial systems.

Finally, the psychological effects of dependence on fiat currency significantly influence consumer behavior in various ways. As individuals become increasingly aware of the inherent limitations and vulnerabilities of fiat systems, they may start to reconsider and reevaluate their financial decisions and investment strategies more critically. Educational outreach initiatives that focus on the underlying technology behind Bitcoin, such as blockchain and decentralization, can effectively demystify this digital asset, encouraging a broader and more diverse audience to engage with it proactively and thoughtfully. By disseminating comprehensive knowledge about Bitcoin's potential to replace traditional monetary systems, advocates can cultivate a more informed and educated investor base that is not only equipped to navigate the complexities of the financial landscape but also empowered to leverage Bitcoin as a valuable tool for achieving economic resilience in an ever-evolving economic environment.

Chapter 10: Understanding Bitcoin Technology

Blockchain Technology: The Foundation of Bitcoin

Blockchain technology serves as the essential backbone of Bitcoin, enabling its decentralized and highly secure nature. At its very core, blockchain functions as a distributed ledger that meticulously records all transactions across a vast network of computers, rendering it virtually tamper-proof and highly reliable. This groundbreaking technology effectively eliminates the need for a central authority, such as a bank or government, to validate and oversee transactions. Instead, it relies on a sophisticated consensus mechanism among network participants, which ensures both transparency and trust among all parties involved. As Bitcoin gained immense popularity over the years, it clearly illustrated how a decentralized system could operate independently of traditional financial institutions, thereby fundamentally challenging the very foundation of fiat currencies and reshaping our understanding of money and value in the modern world.

The evolution of money has undergone a significant transformation, transitioning from the era of tangible assets like gold to the rise of digital currencies such as Bitcoin. This shift has been largely driven by the inherent limitations and weaknesses associated with fiat money. Historically, gold was widely regarded as a reliable store of value due to its scarcity, durability, and intrinsic worth that people recognized and trusted. However, as governments began to issue fiat currencies, which are not backed by physical commodities, the intrinsic value of money diminished. This shift has led to inflation and a gradual loss of purchasing power for individuals. The overprinting of fiat money, often a response to economic crises and attempts to stimulate growth, has resulted in severe hyperinflation in some countries, underscoring the vulnerabilities and risks inherent in traditional monetary systems. In stark contrast to this troubling trend, Bitcoin has been designed as a deflationary asset, offering a compelling solution for investors who are seeking greater stability and security in their financial investments amidst the uncertainties of traditional currencies.

Inflation poses a significant threat to consumers who rely on fiat currency, as it steadily erodes purchasing power over time. Many individuals have unfortunately witnessed their savings diminish in value due to the continuous rise in prices, which has prompted a widespread search for alternative stores of value. In this context, Bitcoin, with its capped supply of 21 million coins, emerges as a compelling hedge against inflation. Real-world case studies from countries grappling with hyperinflation, such as Venezuela, vividly demonstrate how Bitcoin has provided a crucial avenue for citizens to preserve their wealth and maintain their financial stability. Investors and crypto enthusiasts alike increasingly recognize that as traditional fiat systems falter, Bitcoin emerges as a viable alternative, showcasing its potential as a stable asset amidst ongoing economic turmoil and uncertainty. This growing recognition underscores the importance of considering innovative financial solutions in an ever-changing economic landscape.

The policies implemented by central banks play a vital and critical role in determining the valuation of fiat currencies, often leading to various inflationary pressures that can affect the economy. Central banks, which are specifically tasked with managing monetary policy, have frequently found it necessary to resort to quantitative easing and other measures designed to increase the overall money supply. This practice of expanding the money supply can ultimately lead to a significant devaluation of currency, as well as a notable loss of consumer confidence in the financial system. In contrast, Bitcoin operates entirely outside the control of any central authority or institution, providing a more predictable monetary policy that is governed solely by its underlying code. This fundamental difference in how Bitcoin functions positions it as a potential hedge against the unpredictable and often volatile nature of fiat currencies, especially during times of heightened inflationary pressures.

Grassroots movements advocating for Bitcoin adoption are gaining significant traction, particularly in hyperinflationary economies where traditional financial systems have repeatedly failed to provide stability. These movements emphasize a growing awareness among the populace regarding the limitations and vulnerabilities of fiat currencies, as well as the numerous advantages offered by decentralized finance. As an increasing number of individuals turn to Bitcoin as a reliable means of conducting transactions and preserving their wealth, the psychological effects stemming from a dependency on fiat currency are becoming increasingly evident. Investors should carefully consider the broader implications of this transformative shift and the potential for Bitcoin to ultimately replace traditional monetary systems in the not-so-distant future. Gaining a deep understanding of the technology that underpins Bitcoin, as well as its far-reaching implications for economic stability and innovation, will be crucial for those navigating the rapidly evolving landscape of modern finance and investment opportunities.

Decentralization: Implications for Trust and Security

Decentralization fundamentally transforms the landscape of trust and security in financial systems, especially when examining Bitcoin in contrast to traditional fiat currencies. Conventional fiat systems are heavily dependent on centralized authorities, including governments and banks, which are responsible for managing currency supply and ensuring economic stability. However, these institutions have frequently been plagued by issues such as overreach, mismanagement, and a significant lack of accountability, which in turn breeds mistrust among consumers and investors alike. On the other hand, Bitcoin functions on a decentralized blockchain network, where trust is distributed among a vast array of participants, each playing a role in maintaining the integrity of the system. This paradigm shift not only significantly enhances transparency but also effectively mitigates the risks associated with centralized control, including corruption and the potential for arbitrary monetary policies that can adversely impact the economy and individual financial wellbeing.

The implications of decentralization extend far beyond just financial transactions; they reach into the realm of security as well. In traditional fiat systems, the security of one's funds relies heavily on the integrity and reliability of central institutions. Unfortunately, these institutions can be susceptible to various threats such as hacks, fraud, and systemic failures that can jeopardize the safety of user assets. In contrast, decentralized systems like Bitcoin employ advanced cryptographic protocols specifically designed to secure transactions and safeguard against unauthorized access. Every single transaction is meticulously verified by a robust network of nodes, which makes it exceedingly challenging for any single entity to manipulate or compromise the system's integrity. This heightened level of security not only protects the assets of users but also fosters a greater sense of confidence among them. This is particularly crucial in environments where traditional banking systems have a history of being unreliable or insecure, making decentralization an attractive alternative for many individuals seeking financial security.

Moreover, the decentralized nature of Bitcoin significantly fosters a more inclusive financial ecosystem, expanding access to individuals who have previously faced barriers. In hyperinflationary economies or regions characterized by unstable banking infrastructures, people can gain access to essential financial services without relying on a trusted intermediary, which is often scarce in such situations. This empowerment can be particularly transformative for those who have historically been marginalized and excluded from traditional banking systems. By enabling direct peer-to-peer transactions, Bitcoin not only effectively circumvents the numerous inefficiencies associated with fiat currencies but also provides users with significantly greater control over their assets. This increased control ultimately enhances their financial autonomy and independence, allowing them to participate more fully in the global economy.

The psychological effects of decentralization also deserve thorough consideration. In a fiat-dependent society, consumers frequently find themselves at the mercy of central banks and their often unpredictable policies, which can instill a profound sense of helplessness and frustration in the face of persistent inflationary pressures. Decentralization, however, presents a powerful alternative that offers individuals a renewed sense of agency and control over their financial futures. By making the conscious choice to utilize Bitcoin, individuals can actively engage in a monetary system that aligns with their core values of transparency, fairness, and personal empowerment. This transformative shift in mindset not only fosters a broader acceptance of alternative financial systems but also encourages a decisive rejection of traditional fiat dependency, ultimately driving the increased adoption of Bitcoin as a legitimate and viable currency for the modern world.

In conclusion, the decentralization inherent in Bitcoin presents a remarkably compelling alternative to the centralized structures of traditional fiat currencies, particularly in terms of trust and security. As investors and crypto enthusiasts navigate the increasingly complex landscape of modern finance, understanding these implications becomes not just important but crucial for making informed decisions. The shift towards decentralization effectively addresses the numerous shortcomings of fiat money, while also fostering a revolutionary new paradigm in which individuals can reclaim and solidify control over their financial destinies. As we witness the ongoing evolution of money in this digital age, the role of decentralization in shaping a more secure and trustworthy financial future is not only significant but truly cannot be overstated.

The Future of Blockchain Beyond Bitcoin

The future of blockchain technology extends far beyond just Bitcoin, presenting transformative possibilities across a wide array of sectors. While Bitcoin has firmly established itself as a leading digital currency and a reliable hedge against inflation, the underlying blockchain technology holds a wealth of applications that can revolutionize numerous industries, including finance, supply chain management, healthcare, and governance. This innovative decentralized ledger technology enables transparent, tamper-proof transactions that significantly enhance trust and efficiency in processes that have traditionally relied heavily on intermediaries and third parties. As blockchain technology continues to mature and evolve, its immense potential to disrupt conventional systems and create entirely new economic models becomes increasingly evident and undeniable. The implications of these advancements are profound, suggesting a future where blockchain could fundamentally alter the way we conduct business and interact within various sectors.

In the realm of finance, the introduction of blockchain technology has the potential to facilitate not only faster but also significantly cheaper cross-border transactions. This innovation reduces the reliance on costly intermediaries such as banks, which often add layers of complexity and expense. Furthermore, smart contracts, defined as self-executing contracts where the terms of the agreement are directly embedded into code, can efficiently automate and enforce agreements. This capability helps to minimize the risk of human error and fraud, which can plague traditional contract processes. As these revolutionary innovations continue to gain traction, they have the potential to democratize access to financial services, especially in regions where traditional banking infrastructure is lacking or nonexistent. By doing so, they enable unbanked populations to participate actively in the global economy and gain access to essential financial tools. As these applications develop and become more widely adopted, the financial landscape may undergo a dramatic transformation, ultimately providing consumers with enhanced control over their assets and financial futures.

The influence of central bank policies on fiat currencies underscores the urgent necessity for viable alternatives such as Bitcoin and blockchain technology. Central banks frequently engage in quantitative easing and other inflationary tactics, which ultimately lead to the devaluation of fiat money and significantly diminish consumers' purchasing power throughout the economy. In stark contrast, Bitcoin presents a deflationary model characterized by a limited supply, positioning it as a more attractive choice for investors who seek a reliable safeguard against the inflationary pressures imposed by central banks. As public awareness of these critical issues continues to expand, the demand for innovative blockchain-based solutions is anticipated to increase substantially. This trend reinforces the notion that Bitcoin is merely the beginning of a much larger and more transformative blockchain revolution that is actively unfolding in our society today. The emergence of these technologies may pave the way for a new financial landscape that prioritizes stability and transparency.

Additionally, grassroots movements advocating for Bitcoin adoption in hyperinflationary economies are already demonstrating how blockchain can serve as a crucial lifeline for individuals facing the dire consequences of economic collapse. Countries experiencing severe inflation are witnessing a growing and significant interest in Bitcoin as a stable store of value, as people seek alternatives to their rapidly depreciating national currencies. This trend not only highlights the practical applications of blockchain technology in preserving wealth but also underscores its remarkable potential to empower communities and foster economic resilience in challenging times. As these movements gain traction and momentum, they could pave the way for even more widespread acceptance and integration of blockchain solutions into everyday life, ultimately transforming the financial landscape for many individuals.

As we look to the future, blockchain technology is poised to fundamentally transform traditional monetary systems in profound and unprecedented ways. Investors and crypto enthusiasts who are venturing beyond Bitcoin should carefully take into account the various effects of decentralization, increased transparency, and greater security that blockchain offers. The transition from gold to Bitcoin, alongside the persistent challenges posed by fiat currency, marks a significant and pivotal moment in the ongoing evolution of money itself. By fully grasping and effectively leveraging the comprehensive potential of blockchain technology, stakeholders can strategically position themselves at the leading edge of this transformative period. This not only fosters innovation but also significantly influences the future landscape of finance and beyond, unlocking new opportunities that were previously unimaginable.

Chapter 11: Psychological Effects of Fiat Dependency

Consumer Habits and Fiat Money

Consumer behavior in relation to fiat currency is heavily influenced by the systemic flaws that are deeply embedded within the fiat monetary system. As fiat currencies are subject to the whims of central banks and government policies, consumers find themselves often vulnerable to inflationary pressures that can significantly erode their purchasing power over time. The historical evolution of money reveals a stark contrast between fiat currencies and tangible assets like gold, which have consistently retained their value throughout history. This significant shift from a gold-backed standard to fiat systems has created an environment where money is increasingly viewed not as a stable and reliable store of value, but rather as a transient tool that can fluctuate in worth based on external economic factors. The implications of this shift are profound, as they shape consumer confidence and decision-making in complex economic landscapes.

The incessant and often excessive overprinting of fiat currency has inevitably led to rampant and persistent inflation, which directly and significantly impacts consumer behavior in various ways. As the value of money diminishes over time, consumers tend to alter their spending habits, often opting to purchase goods and services sooner rather than later in order to avoid future price increases that are anticipated. This reactive and somewhat impulsive approach to spending can exacerbate inflationary cycles, creating a self-fulfilling prophecy in which spikes in demand lead to further price hikes and increased costs for consumers. Understanding this complex dynamic is crucial for investors, as it underscores the inherent fragility of fiat systems and the growing potential for alternative currencies to provide a more stable and reliable economic foundation.

Bitcoin is increasingly recognized as an appealing alternative to traditional fiat currency, especially as a reliable safeguard against the pressures of rising inflation. Numerous real-world instances clearly demonstrate how individuals and entire communities in hyperinflationary regions have successfully turned to Bitcoin as a means to protect their wealth. In countries such as Venezuela and Zimbabwe, where local currencies have experienced dramatic collapses, Bitcoin has emerged as a crucial support system for financial stability. It has enabled consumers to conduct transactions using a stable digital asset, thereby offering essential financial security in uncertain times. These circumstances underscore not only Bitcoin's versatility as a method of exchange and a store of value but also its significant role in scenarios where conventional fiat systems fail to adequately shield consumers from the adverse effects of economic instability. The ability of Bitcoin to serve as a reliable financial alternative has become increasingly vital in today's ever-changing economic landscape.

Central bank policies play an incredibly pivotal role in determining the value of fiat currencies, often leading to significant and sometimes profound market distortions. When central banks engage in quantitative easing or similar practices, the immediate and observable effect can be an inflated asset bubble, impacting everything from real estate to stocks in various ways. For investors, understanding how these policies influence consumer behavior and purchasing power is absolutely essential for making informed and strategic decisions in the marketplace. A comprehensive comparative analysis of Bitcoin against traditional investments during inflationary periods reveals that Bitcoin often outperforms its counterparts, as it is not directly influenced by the manipulations and interventions of central banks, making it an attractive alternative for those seeking to hedge against inflation.

The rise of grassroots movements advocating for Bitcoin adoption in economies suffering from severe hyperinflation further illustrates the rapidly evolving landscape of consumer behavior and financial attitudes. As individuals increasingly become disillusioned with traditional fiat currency, the psychological dependence on these established systems diminishes significantly, giving way to a growing acceptance and embrace of decentralized currencies like Bitcoin. The underlying technology behind Bitcoin, firmly anchored in blockchain innovation and the principles of decentralization, empowers consumers by providing a transparent, secure, and efficient alternative to conventional monetary systems that have often failed them. Looking ahead, the potential for Bitcoin to effectively replace fiat currencies is not merely a theoretical discussion confined to academic circles; rather, it is becoming an increasingly realistic and tangible prospect as consumers actively seek stability and reliability in a world marked by persistent monetary instability and economic uncertainty.

The Effect of Inflation on Consumer Spending Patterns

The impact of inflation on spending habits is an increasingly critical concern for both investors and crypto enthusiasts alike, especially in light of the deteriorating purchasing power of fiat currency. Inflation steadily erodes the value of money, prompting consumers to adapt their spending behaviors in direct response to the relentless rise in prices. This shift in consumer behavior can manifest in various ways, including prioritizing essential goods, actively seeking out more affordable alternatives, or even delaying purchases altogether to avoid overspending. As inflation continues to rise, driven by excessive money printing and an oversupply of fiat currencies flooding the market, consumers find themselves navigating an increasingly complex financial landscape. In this environment, their money buys less over time, compelling them to carefully reevaluate and adjust their financial strategies to ensure they can maintain their purchasing power and financial stability amidst these challenging conditions.

Historically, the evolution of money has progressed from gold to fiat currencies and now to cryptocurrencies like Bitcoin, reflecting an ongoing struggle against inflationary pressures that affect economies. Gold, cherished for its scarcity and intrinsic value, has served as a reliable store of wealth for centuries, enduring through various economic cycles. However, the shift to fiat currency introduced significant risks associated with inflation, where government policies and central bank decisions can dilute the value of money at will, often leading to economic instability. As fiat systems increasingly fail to preserve their purchasing power, many consumers and investors are now looking toward Bitcoin and other cryptocurrencies. Bitcoin, in particular, offers a fixed supply and a decentralized framework that protects it from the inflationary practices typically employed by central banks, positioning it as an appealing alternative for those seeking to safeguard their wealth.

Inflation has a profound and significant effect on purchasing power, particularly as consumers confront the harsh realities of rising prices in their daily lives. The traditional fiat system has consistently demonstrated a concerning trend of failing to adequately protect consumers from the damaging impacts of inflation, which has led to increased financial stress and anxiety among individuals and families. This situation has prompted a growing interest in alternative assets, with Bitcoin emerging as a particularly attractive option that many view as a reliable hedge against inflation. Real-world case studies provide compelling evidence of how Bitcoin has performed during various inflationary periods, often outpacing traditional investments and providing a robust safeguard for wealth preservation. As consumers become increasingly aware of these economic dynamics, their spending habits are shifting toward assets that promise not only greater stability but also the potential for significant appreciation over time.

Central bank policies play an essential and pivotal role in shaping and determining the value of fiat currency, and their frequent and often aggressive interventions can significantly exacerbate inflationary trends across economies. The reliance on monetary policy as a primary tool to stimulate economic growth often results in an overabundance of money supply, which, in turn, further diminishes the purchasing power of consumers and erodes savings. This ongoing and troubling cycle of inflation has given rise to grassroots movements that strongly advocate for the adoption of Bitcoin, particularly in hyperinflationary environments where fiat currencies have lost their value entirely and become virtually worthless. As individuals increasingly seek out alternatives that offer both reliability and resilience in the face of economic uncertainty, Bitcoin emerges as a compelling and viable solution amidst systemic failures and widespread distrust in traditional financial systems.

In a comprehensive comparative analysis of Bitcoin and traditional investments during inflationary periods, it becomes increasingly evident that Bitcoin offers several distinct advantages that set it apart. While traditional assets, such as stocks and bonds, often struggle to maintain their value amid rising prices and economic uncertainty, Bitcoin's unique properties as a decentralized digital currency present an exceptional opportunity for both growth and protection against inflationary pressures. A deeper understanding of the technology behind Bitcoin, including the fundamentals of blockchain and its decentralized nature, empowers consumers to make well-informed decisions regarding their investments. As the psychological effects of dependence on fiat currency continue to significantly influence consumer behavior and spending patterns, there is a growing recognition within financial circles that Bitcoin could potentially replace traditional monetary systems altogether, fundamentally reshaping spending habits and investment strategies in the process. This potential shift underscores the importance of adapting to new financial paradigms in an ever-evolving economic landscape.

Shifting Mindsets: Embracing Bitcoin

Shifting mindsets towards embracing Bitcoin requires a profound and nuanced understanding of the inherent flaws that exist within fiat currency systems. Over the past century, fiat money has repeatedly demonstrated its vulnerabilities, particularly highlighted by rampant inflation resulting from excessive printing and an overwhelming oversupply of currency. Unlike traditional currencies, which are often subject to the unpredictable whims of central banks and government policies, Bitcoin operates on a decentralized network that imposes a strict limit on its total supply, capping it at 21 million coins. This fixed supply closely mimics the scarcity characteristic of gold, thus providing a compelling argument for Bitcoin as a more stable and reliable store of value. Investors and crypto enthusiasts must come to recognize that the current monetary system is fundamentally broken, and that Bitcoin presents a viable alternative that has the potential to redefine and transform our understanding of what money truly is in the modern world.

The historical evolution of money profoundly highlights the significant transition from gold to fiat currencies, and now, to Bitcoin. For many centuries, gold served as a highly trusted medium of exchange and an effective store of value, largely due to its intrinsic qualities and limited supply. However, the shift to fiat currency in the 20th century marked the beginning of a revolutionary new era in financial systems, characterized by a heavy reliance on government-backed money that can be printed at will, often without any real backing. This fundamental shift has led to considerable economic instability and a persistent loss of purchasing power for consumers worldwide. As we witness the ongoing decline of fiat currencies globally, Bitcoin emerges as a compelling modern solution that reintroduces the essential principles of scarcity and sound money. This development encourages investors and individuals alike to critically reconsider their financial strategies and approaches in an increasingly uncertain economic landscape.

Inflation remains a persistent and significant threat to consumer purchasing power, and throughout history, fiat currency has repeatedly failed to effectively protect individuals from its adverse effects. As central banks around the world adopt increasingly aggressive monetary policies, which include measures such as quantitative easing and maintaining low-interest rates, the value of fiat currency continues to decline. This ongoing devaluation erodes savings and diminishes overall financial security for many individuals. In contrast, Bitcoin's decentralized nature and its fixed supply make it inherently resistant to the pressures of inflation. Numerous real-world case studies illustrate how individuals living in hyperinflationary economies have successfully turned to Bitcoin as a means of preserving their wealth. These examples showcase Bitcoin's potential to serve as a reliable hedge against economic instability and inflationary risks, providing individuals with an alternative avenue for safeguarding their financial futures.

Central bank policies significantly impact the value of fiat currencies, often leading to a wide range of unpredictable economic consequences that can affect markets and consumer behavior. The reliance on monetary policy to stimulate economic growth can create financial bubbles and exacerbate social inequalities, prompting many investors to actively seek alternative assets as a hedge against instability. In contrast, Bitcoin operates independently of central bank influences, offering a transparent and predictable monetary system that appeals to those wary of traditional financial mechanisms. During inflationary periods, Bitcoin has demonstrated remarkable resilience compared to various traditional investments, making it an increasingly attractive option for individuals looking to safeguard their assets in uncertain times. By thoroughly analyzing historical data and trends, investors can clearly see Bitcoin's potential as a strategic tool during times of economic turmoil and volatility, reinforcing its role in modern financial strategies.

The psychological effects of dependence on fiat currency profoundly influence consumer behavior, often leading to a troubling complacency in the face of worsening economic conditions. Grassroots movements that advocate for the adoption of Bitcoin in hyperinflationary economies underscore a growing awareness of these critical issues and a strong desire for meaningful change. As an increasing number of individuals begin to recognize the inherent limitations and vulnerabilities of fiat currencies, the desire for a decentralized alternative, such as Bitcoin, continues to gain significant traction and support. Understanding the sophisticated technology behind Bitcoin, including the concepts of blockchain and decentralization, empowers both investors and enthusiasts alike to fully embrace this transformative shift in mindset. This collective awakening could pave the way for a future where Bitcoin not only complements but potentially replaces traditional monetary systems entirely, creating a new paradigm for financial interactions and economic stability.

Chapter 12: Future Predictions for Bitcoin

Bitcoin's Place in the Evolving Monetary Landscape

Bitcoin's emergence as a prominent alternative to fiat currency marks a significant and transformative shift in the ever-evolving landscape of monetary systems. Throughout history, the concept of money has undergone considerable transitions, moving from tangible assets such as gold and silver to increasingly abstract forms of currency, which culminates in the innovative digital representation of value that Bitcoin offers today. This remarkable evolution reflects a growing disillusionment with traditional fiat systems, particularly as they struggle with rampant inflation and the far-reaching consequences resulting from excessive money printing and unsustainable fiscal policies. Investors and crypto enthusiasts alike increasingly recognize that Bitcoin, with its limited supply and decentralized nature, stands in stark and compelling contrast to the inflationary pressures that consistently plague traditional currencies and financial systems. The allure of Bitcoin lies not only in its potential for value appreciation but also in its promise of a more stable and resilient financial future.

The failures of fiat currency systems have become glaringly apparent, particularly in the context of rising inflation rates that significantly erode purchasing power for individuals and families alike. As central banks around the world continue to inject vast amounts of liquidity into their economies in an attempt to stimulate growth, the value of fiat currency diminishes further, leading consumers to confront increasingly higher prices for essential goods and services. This troubling scenario underscores the fundamental weaknesses inherent in fiat currency systems, where trust in government institutions and the efficacy of monetary policy becomes increasingly precarious and questionable over time. In contrast, Bitcoin's fixed supply of 21 million coins presents a compelling argument for its consideration as a stable store of value, offering a potential safeguard for purchasing power in an environment that is increasingly characterized by financial instability and uncertainty.

Numerous real-world case studies compellingly illustrate Bitcoin's remarkable effectiveness as a hedge against inflation, particularly in countries grappling with severe hyperinflation. In troubled places like Venezuela and Zimbabwe, where local currencies have dramatically lost their value almost overnight, Bitcoin has emerged as a vital lifeline, enabling individuals to preserve their wealth and actively engage in international trade with greater ease. The grassroots movements passionately advocating for Bitcoin adoption in these economies underscore its significant role as a means of financial empowerment in the face of oppressive and often unpredictable monetary policies. As a result, investors are increasingly encouraged to view Bitcoin not merely as a speculative asset but as a practical and innovative solution for those adversely affected by the inherent flaws and instability of fiat currency systems. This shift in perspective can open up new avenues for financial security and independence in challenging economic landscapes.

Central bank policies play a crucial role in shaping the value of fiat currencies, often leading to unintended consequences that can significantly contribute to economic crises and instability. The response to financial downturns frequently involves expansive monetary policies, which further dilute the currency's value and can erode public confidence in the financial system. In contrast, Bitcoin operates independently of such manipulations and interventions, providing a decentralized alternative that effectively challenges the status quo of traditional finance. A thorough comparative analysis of Bitcoin against traditional investments during inflationary periods reveals that Bitcoin has consistently outperformed many assets, showcasing its resilience and potential as a safe haven for investors who are seeking stability amid chaos and uncertainty in the marketplace. This performance emphasizes the growing appeal of Bitcoin as a viable investment option in turbulent economic times.

Looking ahead, the potential for Bitcoin to replace traditional monetary systems seems increasingly plausible and even inevitable. As technology continues to advance at a rapid pace and public awareness of Bitcoin's numerous advantages grows steadily, its role in the global economy could evolve significantly and fundamentally. The psychological dependence on fiat currency has created a complex landscape where consumer behavior is heavily influenced by trust in central banks and various government policies. However, as more individuals and institutions begin to recognize the substantial benefits of decentralization and the remarkable transparency offered by blockchain technology, the adoption of Bitcoin is likely to accelerate even further. In this broader context, Bitcoin stands not only as a financial instrument but also as a revolutionary force poised to reshape the entire monetary landscape for generations to come, potentially offering a more equitable and resilient financial system.

Potential for Bitcoin to Replace Traditional Systems

The potential for Bitcoin to fundamentally replace traditional financial systems is deeply rooted in its unique characteristics as a decentralized currency that stands in stark contrast to the conventional fiat monetary system. Fiat currencies are inherently susceptible to inflation because of their reliance on central banks that have the authority to print money at will, often without sufficient backing. This excessive production of money frequently leads to a significant devaluation of purchasing power, which adversely affects consumers and their ability to maintain their standard of living. As inflation rates continue to soar and erode the value of money, the need for a stable and reliable alternative becomes increasingly urgent for individuals and businesses alike. Bitcoin, with its capped supply of 21 million coins and its deflationary nature, presents an attractive and viable solution for investors and crypto enthusiasts alike who are actively seeking protection against the erosion of value that consistently plagues traditional fiat currencies.

Historically, the evolution of money has progressed from tangible assets such as gold to modern fiat currencies, with each significant step being influenced by the changing needs of society and the advancements in technology. Gold has long been regarded as a reliable store of value due to its inherent scarcity and intrinsic worth, making it a preferred medium of exchange for centuries. However, the transition to fiat money has allowed for greater flexibility in monetary policy, which in turn has fueled economic growth and adaptability. Yet, this newfound flexibility has also led to the potential pitfalls of inflation and economic instability, clearly demonstrating the inherent flaws in a system that relies heavily on trust in governments and central banks to manage currency effectively. In this context, Bitcoin emerges as the next logical step in the ongoing evolution of money, presenting a digital alternative that is not only scarce but also decentralized. This innovative form of currency has the potential to redefine what constitutes sound money in the modern era, challenging traditional notions and practices in the financial landscape.

The failure of fiat currencies to maintain their purchasing power significantly highlights their inadequacy, especially during times of economic distress. Inflation systematically erodes consumer wealth, leading to a vicious cycle in which individuals are forced to spend increasingly larger amounts of money to acquire the same goods and services they once could purchase for less. In stark contrast, the unique structure of Bitcoin enables it to function as an effective hedge against inflation, with numerous case studies providing compelling evidence of its resilience during hyperinflationary periods. Countries like Venezuela and Zimbabwe have experienced a marked surge in Bitcoin adoption, as citizens desperately seek refuge from their collapsing local currencies and the economic turmoil that accompanies such instability. These real-world examples powerfully underscore the urgent need for a viable alternative to traditional fiat currencies, positioning Bitcoin not merely as a speculative asset but also as a practical and potentially transformative solution in the face of economic challenges.

Central bank policies significantly influence the value of fiat currencies, often resulting in adverse effects on the broader economy. The manipulation of interest rates and the practice of quantitative easing can create artificial economic environments that ultimately lead to significant market distortions. As central banks persist in their implementation of expansive monetary policies, the inherent risks associated with fiat currency systems become increasingly pronounced and evident. In contrast, Bitcoin's decentralized nature effectively mitigates many of these systemic risks, providing a transparent alternative that operates independently of any government interference or control. This fundamental shift in the dynamics of monetary control has the potential to lead to a more stable and resilient economic landscape, offering investors a new and compelling avenue for wealth preservation and growth in uncertain times.

Grassroots movements advocating for Bitcoin adoption in hyperinflationary economies reflect a growing and widespread recognition of its transformative potential. As consumers increasingly become disillusioned with traditional financial systems, the demand for a decentralized currency continues to rise significantly. Understanding the technology behind Bitcoin, particularly its blockchain and decentralized framework, is crucial and essential for both investors and enthusiasts alike. The psychological effects of fiat currency dependence can lead to a dangerous complacency in financial decision-making, but the rise of Bitcoin encourages a far more proactive and engaged approach to wealth management. Looking ahead, numerous predictions suggest that Bitcoin's role as a viable alternative to traditional monetary systems will only strengthen and expand, as more individuals and communities actively embrace its potential to foster economic resilience, independence, and empowerment.

The Role of Regulation in Bitcoin's Future

The future of Bitcoin is inextricably linked to the evolving regulatory landscape that emerges around it. As Bitcoin continues to gain significant traction as a prominent alternative to traditional fiat currency, the role of regulation becomes increasingly pivotal in shaping its long-term trajectory. Investors, as well as crypto enthusiasts, must recognize that regulatory frameworks can either foster innovation and broad adoption or stifle growth and limit access to this revolutionary technology. Effective and well-thought-out regulation can instill a sense of confidence among users and investors alike by providing a clear and comprehensive set of rules. This clarity helps in reducing the inherent risks associated with volatility and fraud that often plague the cryptocurrency market. Conversely, overly restrictive measures could hinder development and push innovation underground, ultimately undermining the potential of Bitcoin to serve as a viable monetary system in the future. It is crucial for stakeholders to engage in constructive dialogue with regulators to ensure that the emerging rules support a balanced approach that encourages both innovation and consumer protection.

Historically, regulations have evolved alongside advancements in technology and changes in financial systems, frequently in response to various crises. The ascent of Bitcoin has compelled governments and financial institutions to confront its far-reaching implications for monetary policy and overall economic stability. For example, as central banks globally grapple with the persistent challenges of inflation driven by excessive money printing practices, the emergence of Bitcoin as a decentralized and inherently deflationary asset presents an alternative that has the potential to significantly disrupt established monetary frameworks. Policymakers are faced with the complex task of balancing the imperative to protect consumers and ensure financial stability while simultaneously recognizing that Bitcoin might serve as a viable hedge against the very inflationary pressures they are working to control and mitigate. This delicate balance requires careful consideration and thoughtful regulation to navigate the evolving landscape.

The impact of regulation on Bitcoin is particularly significant in hyperinflationary economies, where grassroots movements advocating for Bitcoin adoption are gaining significant momentum and visibility. In countries that are suffering from severe currency devaluation and a dramatic loss of purchasing power, Bitcoin emerges as a crucial lifeline for individuals who are actively seeking to preserve their wealth and financial stability. Regulatory clarity can greatly empower these movements, providing essential legal protection for users and businesses that are operating within the Bitcoin ecosystem. On the other hand, if restrictive regulations are imposed, they could force these initiatives underground, severely limiting the ability of citizens to access and utilize Bitcoin as a vital safeguard against overwhelming economic instability and uncertainty.

Moreover, the in-depth comparative analysis of Bitcoin in relation to traditional investments during inflationary periods clearly highlights the pressing need for a supportive regulatory environment. Historically, Bitcoin has demonstrated an ability to outperform a variety of traditional assets, including stocks and bonds, particularly during times of significant economic distress. This impressive performance not only underscores the value of Bitcoin as an investment alternative but also emphasizes the critical importance of establishing regulations that serve a dual purpose: protecting investors while simultaneously encouraging the seamless integration of Bitcoin into mainstream financial systems. Thoughtfully crafted regulations that promote transparency and ensure robust investor protection can play a vital role in legitimizing

Bitcoin, ultimately facilitating its broader acceptance as a standard asset class that stands alongside traditional investments.

Looking ahead, the role of regulation will be absolutely crucial in determining whether Bitcoin can genuinely replace traditional monetary systems that have been in place for decades. As the landscape of digital currencies continues to evolve rapidly, it is imperative that policymakers develop a deep understanding of the technology behind Bitcoin. This includes grasping the fundamental principles of blockchain and decentralization, which are critical to its functionality and success, in order to create effective regulatory frameworks. By fostering a regulatory environment that not only encourages innovation but also prioritizes the safeguarding of consumer interests, regulators can play a pivotal role in helping Bitcoin realize its full potential as a viable and robust alternative to traditional fiat currency. This delicate balance between innovation and protection will ultimately shape the future of finance, impacting both investors and consumers in profound and transformative ways, as we move towards a more digital financial landscape.

www.ingramcontent.com/pod-product-compliance
Lightning Source LLC
Chambersburg PA
CBHW071028240526
45469CB00006BD/2137